THREE PLAYS BY JOHN F LEVIN

THREE PLAYS BY JOHN F. LEVIN

VERACRUZ

SNOWBIRDS

BIG MONEY

BLACK APOLLO PRESS
First edition, 2015

ISBN: 9781900355834

Copyright © John F. Levin 2015

A CIP catalogue record of this book is available at the British Library.

All rights reserved; no part of this publication may be reproduced or transmitted by any means electronic, mechanical, photocopying or otherwise without the prior permission of the author.

Germinal Productions, Ltd
www.blackapollopress.com

Cover Design: Kevin Biderman

CONTENTS

VERACRUZ	7
SNOWBIRDS	80
BIG MONEY	136

For Paula

VERACRUZ

INTRODUCTION

On April 21, 1914 the United States, seeking to control Mexico's natural resources, particularly its oil reserves, occupied Mexico's port city of Veracruz. Most people in the United States and the world thought that the occupation of Veracruz was only a first step in what would be a full scale invasion and probable annexation of most if not all of Mexico. Reporters, adventurers and entrepreneurs from all over the world flocked to Veracruz for a ringside seat at the beginning of the American Empire.

SCENES

Prologue

Act One

Scene One: *Portales Café, Hotel Diligencias*
Scene Two: *The Londons' Quarters, Hotel Diligencias*
Scene Three: *Portales Café*
Scene Four: *Sor Juana's*

Act Two

Scene One: *Sor Juana's*
Scene Two: *Exterior Sor Juana's*
Scene Three: *The Londons' Quarters*
Scene Four: *The Portales Café*
Scene Five: *The Londons' Quarters*

CAST

Jack London: *38, America's foremost celebrity writer.*
Captain Douglas MacArthur: *34, a bright, awkward man at the beginning of his career.*
Charmian London: *43, Jack's wife and partner.*
Fred Boalt: *20's, a reporter for a socialist wire service.*
Bill Buckley: *50's, a courtly Texas businessman.*
Ensign William "Bully" Richardson: *20's.*
Dick Davis: *40's, a reporter for the Hearst newspapers.*
Walt Shepherd: *50's, a reporter for the Associated Press.*
Sor Juana: *a madam.*
China Girl: *18, a whore.*
Captain Burnside: *30's, U.S. Occupation Government.*

PROLOGUE

As a scratchy, contemporaneous recording of the Irving Berlin song, They're On They're Way To Mexico plays, archival photographs and film footage of the 1914 U.S. Invasion of Veracruz, Mexico are projected onto a scrim.

RECORDING
*THEY'RE GETTING READY, THEY'RE GETTING READY,
WE'VE HAD A ROW AND NOW THEY'RE GOING TO WAR.
THEY'VE GOT THEIR ORDERS TO SAIL THE WATERS
WITH HEAVY HEART THEY START FOR THE FOREIGN SHORE.
THEY'RE NOT EXCITED THEY'RE JUST DELIGHTED
TO GO AND SHAKE THEM AND MAKE THEM STAND UP
AND ROAR LIKE THEY NEVER DID BEFORE.
THEY'RE ON THEIR WAY TO MEXICO!*

*JUST SEE THOSE YANKEE FIGHTERS, FOE EXCITERS
GETTING READY TO GO.
THEY'RE ON THEIR WAY TO WIN THE DAY.
JUST TAKE A LOOK AT THOSE YANKEE BROTHERS WAVING
TO THEIR GRAY HAIR'D MOTHERS.
GOOD-BYE THEY'RE LEAVING;
GOOD-BYE STOP GRIEVING,
DON'T CRY THEY'RE GLAD TO GO.
THEY'LL MAKE THEM RUN LIKE A HERD OF CATTLE,
THEY'LL KNOW THEY'VE HAD SOME BATTLE.
WAY DOWN IN MEXICO!*

*COME ON OVER NEAR THEM; COME ON
AND CHEER THEM!*

THEY'VE GOT A RIGHT TO FIGHT THIS BATTLE BECAUSE THEY'VE BEEN INVITED TO GO AND FIGHT IT
AND SO THEY'RE IN TO WIN AND THEY'LL NEVER PAUSE UNTIL THEY TAKE 'EM
AND THEN THEY'LL MAKE 'EM, WITH HEAD ERECT, RESPECT AMERICAN LAWS.
GIVE THREE CHEERS FOR THEM BECAUSE
THEY'RE ON THEIR WAY TO MEXICO!

VERACRUZ

ACT ONE; SCENE ONE
THE PORTALES - MORNING

Veracruz, May 1, 1914.

It is hot, unimaginably so at the veranda cafe under the portals of the Hotel Diligencias, whose bullet-scarred facade is evidence of the fighting that took place only a week ago. Stage left and right are sandbagged for machine gun emplacements. Two Guests enter from the Hotel and, wiping their brows, take seats at a table for their morning coffee. They are white, large and robust They suffer greatly from the heat and humidity.

Jack London, 38, enters from the hotel, and makes his way along the edge of the tables, carefully keeping in the shade of the hotel. One of the guests points him out.

Jack is short, broad-shouldered, with a muscular body starting to soften around the edges. He wears a freshly pressed white linen suit, a short red kerchief necktie that ends just below his chest emphasizing the nascent curve of his belly.

Richard [Dick] Harding Davis, a portly 42, sits at a table keeping up a steady cadence on a Corona portable. He wears a straw boater with a polka-dot hat band that matches his bow-tie.

Jack spots him and heads in his direction. Tripping, Jack makes a joke out of it, stumbling into the sun and then jumping back as if he bounced out of a frying pan. The guests smile appreciatively.

Jack tips his Stetson to them and collapses into the chair opposite Dick, who continues to type as they talk.

JACK: My head feels like a bull sat on it.
DICK: Nothing quite like a hangover on a humid, tropical morning.

ACT ONE; SCENE ONE

JACK: "Hangover." Who ever coined that never had one. "Crudo!", now that has a mean, bare-knuckled punch. Compañero!

[The waiter enters with a black coffee and a copa of brandy for Jack.]

DICK: "Compañero." Lord, you are a treasure, Jack.

JACK: Saludos!

[Jack knocks back his brandy. The waiter pours Jack a refill and fades back. Jack nurses it with his coffee.
Fred Boalt, 24, dressed in a rumpled, seersucker suit and battered Panama, enters.]

FRED: Jack, could I have a word with you?

JACK: Seat yourself down, Freddie my lad, how you be?

DICK: Dick Davis.

[Dick offers his hand; Fred crosses his arms.]

FRED: I know who you are and I don't like what you write or who you write it for.

JACK: Fred, I've worked along side Dick on three different continents and he's always played a straight hand.

FRED: I don't call glorifying the slaughter of working men for the benefit of capital playing a straight hand.

[Dick notes a new arrival, a young U.S. Army Captain, with an excess of expensive luggage, entering the hotel.]

DICK: If you'll excuse me, one socialist before breakfast is quite enough.

FRED: And proud to call myself one.

DICK*: I'll see you later, Jack--unless you and your compañero run off with Pancho Villa.*

[Dick exits, following the Captain into the Hotel.]

FRED: Hearst's favorite warmonger.

JACK: We're all warmongers; that's why we're here. And, by the way, what's the war news?

VERACRUZ

FRED: Five troopers were wounded last night in a skirmish with a Zapatista squad that tried to breech our lines.

JACK: Or ours, theirs. Wilson started it and he's going to finish it. General Funston probably already has his Mexico City marching orders.

FRED: Jack, I drafted this.

[Fred hands Jack a piece of paper. Jack puts on his spectacles and reads.]

JACK: "HEROIC WORKERS AND CITIZENS OF VERACRUZ:" We salute your just struggle against the guns of American Imperialist Invaders. The guns that have struck down the Heroic Defenders of Veracruz are the same guns that have slain American workers in the mines, mills and factories of the United States. The same bosses that oppress the workers of Veracruz, oppress the American working man as well. Same enemy! Same fight! Yours in Solidarity-- Socialist Party, U.S.A."

FRED: On the other side I'll print your letter.

[Jack looks perplexed. Fred takes the letter out and reads. First Jack recognizes the letter, then he warms to it.]

FRED: "Dear Brave Comrades of the Mexican Revolution: We socialists, anarchists, hoboes, chicken thieves, outlaws and undesirable citizens of the United States are with you heart and soul in your efforts to overthrow slavery and autocracy in Mexico. All the names you are being called, we have been called. And when graft and greed get up and begin to call names, honest men, brave men, patriotic men and martyrs can expect nothing else than to be called chicken thieves and outlaws. I subscribe myself a chicken thief and revolutionist, --Jack London"

JACK: Those were some days, lad?

ACT ONE; SCENE ONE

FRED: 1911 but it could have been written last week. I heard you were with the Wobs when they helped Magón take Mexicali.

[Jack gives a coy shrug and takes Fred's leaflet.]

JACK: You turn a good phrase. "Same enemy; same fight."

FRED: Debs used it in his Homestead speech.

JACK: If you're going to steal, steal from the best. Party give you authorization to put this out in their name?

FRED: How could they?--I'm certainly not going to try to cable them through military censors. There's nothing in it they'd disagree with. Nor Debs for that matter.

[Fred grabs it back, and takes out his pen.]

FRED [*Altering it*]: Fred Boalt, American Socialist Caucus of Veracruz. How's that?

JACK: Fine, if you want to be on the next transport out of here. As soon as that lands on General Funston's desk, there's gonna be your expulsion order coming off it. Mine too if you print that letter.

FRED: It's important that the Mexicans know that not all Americans--

JACK [*Interrupts*]: Most Mexicans can't read; half of them don't even speak Spanish. What that is, Fred, speaking of your petition--now this is comrade-to-comrade, so don't take offense but what your petition is, is an ill-conceived piece of East Coast college boy socialism.

[Before Fred can reply]

There she be, my dearest beloved, now isn't she a welcome sight in the first of the morning?

[Charmian London, 43, a pert short woman in white blouse and gray skirt, carrying a folder, approaches the table. Jack grabs her and pulls her into his lap.]

VERACRUZ

CHARMIAN: Jack, everyone is looking.

JACK *[Tipping his hat in their direction]*: Let them look, let them look, and learn what true and lusty love between she-mate and man-mate is all about.

> *[He gives her a big kiss on the lips and then removes typed sheets from her folder.]*

CHARMIAN: 1248 words. We did a good morning's work, if I do say so.

JACK: Where are the expenses?

CHARMIAN: Last page. I included Nakata's new tropical suit and the sun-dress I bought at Hinks for the trip.

JACK: Good girl. Have them send the remittance to Eliza.

> *[Jack takes the folder, urges her out of his lap and starts editing the copy. Charmian rearranges herself in a convenient chair. Acknowledging Fred, she offers him her hand. She has a hearty grip.]*

CHARMIAN: Charmian London--

FRED: Fred Boalt, Newspaper Enterprise Association.

CHARMIAN: You must be one of Jack's new friends.

FRED: We met last night and found that we share more than the coincidence of being in Veracruz.

CHARMIAN: What is that?

FRED: We both carry the party card.

CHARMIAN: I, too.

FRED: Then I may call you Comrade London?

CHARMIAN: If you want, but our friends call me Charmian.

[To Jack]

Reads pretty good don't you think?

JACK: Good enough for Colliers, most of the readers just look at Jimmy Hare's photos anyway.

ACT ONE; SCENE ONE

CHARMIAN: Not when you're writing for them, mate.

JACK: Have Nakata run it over to the telegraph office.

[Jack slips the copy back into the folder and flips it in her direction. Charmian grabs it, jumps up and mock salutes.]

CHARMIAN: Yes sir, Mr. God Almighty

[To Fred]

That's what our boy, Nakata, calls him when he starts ordering us around.

[Mimicking Nakata]

Yes sir! Mr. God-All-Mighty, yes sir.

[Jack takes a playful slap at her backside as she exits.]

JACK: Off with you, wench!

[To Fred]

I'm a lucky man to have a mate like that. Now tell me, lad, what are you going to do with that screed of yours?

FRED: Jack, maybe you're right but it makes me so damn angry--

JACK: Of course it does; but a fighter has to know how to pick his punches. He may have the best left hook in the world but if he doesn't know when to throw it--it's ass over tea-kettle in the first round. Same with words, Fred, the punch is in their timing.

FRED: I see your point.

JACK: Just some comradely advice.

FRED: And I thank you for it, comrade.

[Fred, deciding, tears it up. Jack starts to leave.]

FRED: Jack, I'm not sure but I think I'm onto something big--something that would show this invasion for what it really is. I heard rumors that the night of the surrender some Mex prisoners were shot--for sport.

JACK *[Impressed]:* Damn Fred, that's a hell of a story. Think you can track it down.

VERACRUZ

FRED: Rumor is that it was a squad off the USS Arkansas--I heard they do their drinking in a pulquería on Calle Rayón. I'm heading there tonight.

[Summoning up the courage]

I was wondering, Jack, if you'd want to work together on it? With your name on it the story would be front page of every paper in the country.

[Dick enters with the army captain, a squarely built man with an awkward but powerful presence. He has a determined delivery as if he edits every sentence.]

JACK: Now that's a thought. Calle Rayón?

FRED: Right off the Malecón.

JACK: I'll meet up with you.

[Jack turns toward Dick.]

DICK: Jack one of our fighting men would like to meet you. Jack London. Captain Douglas MacArthur.

JACK: A pleasure.

FRED: Jack, I'll see you later.

[Fred exits.]

JACK: Have a seat gents. Captain, Coffee? Something stronger?

[They sit down.]

DOUGLAS: No thank you, Mr. London, and please accept my apologies but I prevailed on Mr. Davis to introduce us. I'm a great admirer of yours. I first heard of your books when I served in the Philippines. The men called them jacklondons and passed them around until they fell apart. Men were regularly put on report for reading them on duty.

JACK: Did you have them shot?

DOUGLAS: Worse, we took away their jacklondons.

JACK: Better for it. Fiction reading's a waste of a good man's time.

ACT ONE; SCENE ONE

DOUGLAS: How can you say that, Mr. London?

JACK: I write them; I don't read them. I admit that when I first started out I thought it was something, turning out a good chesty tale but now the best I can say for the writing trade is that it keeps the bill collectors off my ranch. Science. Philosophy. Sociology. Evolution. That's what I would like to write. But Colliers or Hearst won't pay for that, nor will anybody else.

DOUGLAS: If it's your calling, monetary considerations should be put aside.

JACK: My creditors are also calling, but Captain, if you know of any banker who would take philosophy instead of hard cash, my address is Beauty Ranch, Glen Ellen, Sonoma, California, and you tell him I'll meet his train.

DOUGLAS *[...getting it]:* The very first I come across, I'll send him your way, Mr. London.

DICK *[Pointedly]:* Captain MacArthur, I believe you had just joined the General Staff when we met last in Washington. As General Wood's top aide, if I'm not mistaken.

DOUGLAS: I could have no finer mentor.

JACK: General Staff, eh? Then can you tell us about the plans to take Mexico City?

DOUGLAS: I'm just a simple soldier, Mr. London, awaiting orders.

JACK: I don't think that fits you, Captain, but a man's got a right to play his own hand. How long have we been here, Dick? Going on two weeks and to tell you the truth there's nothing much to write about but the weather--and neither Colliers nor Mr. Hearst are paying their war correspondents for weather reports.

[Captain Thomas Burnside enters stage right.]

CAPTAIN BURNSIDE: Douglas, there you are.

[Everybody stands and shake hands around.]

DOUGLAS: Captain Burnside, Mr. London, Mr. Davis.

[To Jack and Dick]

I'm afraid duty calls.

DICK: Cocktails here every evening.

JACK: When the shadow crosses the yardarm.

DICK: Jack taught the muchachos how to shake a dry martini.

DOUGLAS: Then I hope to see you both here this evening.

JACK *[Needling Douglas]:* "God speed to The Heights!" That's always the first toast at the Portales and the second glass is raised to General Winfield Scott, in the hopes they shall soon see his like here again. Do you think they will, Captain?

DOUGLAS *[Giving it back]:* Not likely, if the Socialists have their way. They are rallying public opinion against the president's policy, just the way they did against Fathers' in the Philippines. But you are probably already aware of that Mr. London?

JACK: First I've heard.

DOUGLAS: I've been told that you are of the Socialist persuasion?

JACK *[Unperturbed]:* I stand for socialism but it's different from the Eastern type that you are probably acquainted with.

DOUGLAS: How so Mr. London? I thought it was all pretty much the same hate-the-capitalists crowd.

JACK *[Confidently]:* The exploiters, Captain, the exploiters. I stand for the socialism of the American West that believes that every full blooded laboring man who bends his shoulder ten, twelve nay sixteen hours a day, six--seven days a week to the weal of capital deserves a decent wage, sustenance for his family, and a future for his children. And that includes the twenty-thousand Anglo-Saxon pioneers who settled

ACT ONE; SCENE ONE

this side of the Rio Grande and now wait in refugee camps praying their government will save them.

DOUGLAS: Well that is different, if I understand you correctly. I too feel a sacred obligation to protect our citizens who have settled in this country or any other; and let me assure you that I believe some of the practices of our capitalists are not to be condoned.

DICK *[Sardonic]:* Child Labor.

DOUGLAS: Precisely, Mr. Davis, your mother's book on the subject has a prominent place in my parents' library.

CAPTAIN BURNSIDE: Douglas, we're keeping General Funston waiting.

DOUGLAS *[To Davis]:* I look forward to continuing our discussion. I've always been a great admirer of yours, Mr. Davis.

DICK: I'm flattered.

DOUGLAS: "Remember the Maine!" Simple yet succinct. You captured the nation's heart and gave TR his battle cry, some say the presidency.

[Douglas shakes hands with Dick and then turns to Jack.]

DOUGLAS: Mr. London, it has been an honor.

JACK: Jack, my friends call me Jack.

DOUGLAS: Then it's Douglas here.

[To Captain Burnside]

Thomas, shall we be off?

[Douglas and Captain Burnside exit.]

DICK: "Not the Socialism you're acquainted with." Quite adroit of you, Jack.

[Jack gives Dick a wink and tips his hat in the direction of a woman who enters from the hotel and exits stage left.]

JACK: I'd like to get in her knickers.

DICK: Don't be so crude.

[As Jack reaches over to check.]

JACK: Dick, do you have a pecker?

[Dick slaps his hand away.]

DICK: I have one; but I try not to let it guide my social discourse.

[Jack gives Dick a sarcastic pat on the shoulder and exits into the hotel.]

BLACK OUT

ACT ONE; SCENE TWO
THE LONDONS' QUARTERS

The room is furnished with chairs, a daybed and two writing desks. An interior door leads to a bedroom. Charmian, wearing spectacles, sits at her desk on top of which is a typewriter and a pair of steel scissors, writing in her journal. Plans for the re-building of Wolf House are strewn on Jack's desk. The first page, an architects's drawing of WOLF HOUSE, is pinned to the bullet scarred wall adjacent to the desk.

Stage Left: an open door leads into the bedroom.

Jack enters, tired and in pain. He grabs a bottle of bicarbonate of soda and mixes up a healthy dose.

JACK: Any mail, mate?

CHARMIAN: A packet from Eliza. She sent this.
  [Jack takes a folded poster from her and opens it and reads.]
JACK: "The drink that knocked out John Barleycorn"
  [He displays it: It is a drawing of Jack, his arm around a life-sized bottle labelled "Jack's Grape Juice."]
JACK: Looks like I'm about to give it a kiss.
CHARMIAN: I think you look pretty good.
JACK: I can't think how I could look more ridiculous--maybe if I hired out as a carney geek.
  [Jack's imitation is cut short by a sharp pain in his kidney. He collapses on the sofa; Charmian goes to him.]
JACK *[As it subsides]:* Damn, it's like getting kicked by a mule.
CHARMIAN: Jack, Doctor----
JACK *[Cutting her off]:* Stone is a useless quack.

CHARMIAN: Perhaps he is that, Jack, but every doctor we've consulted has said you must-

JACK *[Interrupting]:* Live a fine upstanding life and go to mass on Sunday.

CHARMIAN: I think you could forego mass...

JACK: What news from Eliza

[Charmian gets up leaving Jack sitting on the day bed.]

CHARMIAN: Eliza said that the check from Mr. Philips was for twelve hundred; not two thousand that you said she should expect.

JACK: I'll cable the Son of a Bitch. Two thousand is what we're owed on publication. I should know, I signed the damn contract.

CHARMIAN: Minus expenses. Eliza had McGrath review the contract. You must have missed that when you signed it.

JACK: Philips could give a Hebrew lessons on how to skin a man.

CHARMIAN: McGrath suggested in the future that you let him review your agreements before you sign them.

JACK: And give him the money instead. I'd as soon hand it over to Philips

CHARMIAN: She also wrote that she got a call from Dewitt's. They said unless we settle our past accounts they'll be no feed delivery next month.

JACK: She can pay them off with the next Collier's check.

CHARMIAN: We've already set that aside for the mortgage. She suggests she try to get them to take four hundred from Philip's check and delay the mortgage which will get us through the next month by which time we'll have four more checks from Colliers.

JACK: What a state eh Mate? Jack London on bent knees praying to the Gods of War so he can pay his mortgage.

ACT ONE; SCENE TWO

CHARMIAN: Jack, you didn't start this war you're only reporting it.

JACK: What other good news from my beloved sister?

CHARMIAN: Two friends of yours showed up at the gate Jack Stanton and Joe Riley.

JACK: Never heard of them.

CHARMIAN: They said they met you when you lectured at the Wobblie Hall in Seattle and that you promised them work if they ever got to Sonoma. She put them to work clearing brush but there's only enough work for a few days.

JACK: Good I want to put in a water tank up there. Did she get the estimate for the Wolf House framing?

CHARMIAN: The lowest bid was ten thousand dollars.

JACK: I swear my sister should have been christened Cassandra.

CHARMIAN: Jack, she is utterly devoted to you.

JACK: Well, maybe we'll see a dime or two from this.

[Jack looks at her for confirmation; she smiles indulgently.]

JACK: Another one of my pipe dreams, eh?

[He tosses the grape juice ad in a wastepaper basket.]

CHARMIAN: Jack, we're carrying twice the hands we need and it's not just the wages but board and-

JACK: I'll be damned if I'll send any of my hands down the hill!

CHARMIAN: If we don't bring the expenses down, we might as well forget about rebuilding Wolf House.

JACK: Never! Strength of the Strong is a top book, a big seller. I'm sure to get $5000 for the movie rights.

CHARMIAN: With the fees you've been paying out to the lawyers, we'll be lucky to be left with half of that.

JACK: Come on mate. I'm making a thousand a week, free and clear, expenses covered.

CHARMIAN: Colliers is paying for Jack London on a war--If

VERACRUZ

General Funston doesn't march on Mexico City--You'll be recalled.

JACK: War or no, I'll get the money for Wolf House. So lets hear no more on that score.

CHARMIAN: Until the sheriff padlocks the ranch gate.

JACK: Truly, Charmian between you and Eliza a man might as well slit his throat.

[A heavy silence...]

JACK: Sometimes I long for when all I had were the clothes on my back and every waking hour wasn't spent in the service of my creditors. I was like that young lad you met downstairs; fighting for The Cause and not a care in the world.

CHARMIAN *[Hurt]:* I like our life together now, mate.

JACK *[Relenting]:* Of course and so do I; so do I. It's hard sometimes getting the truth; and in numbers no less when it is at it's hardest.

[[He smiles reaching out, urging her to join him on the day bed. ...She comes and sits down beside him, he massages her back and neck..]

JACK: We'll get by, we always do. I have a $3000 payment due for the Sea Wolf film rights. That will take care the back mortgage and what we owe the feedlot.

CHARMIAN: We're always so stretched, Jack.

JACK: But never broken, eh?...

CHARMIAN: I guess We're just too clever-

JACK: By half...

CHARMIAN *[arching her back]:* ...Oh that's divine...

JACK: Did I tell you I came up with a damn big idea this morning. I got to thinking about Little Women of the Big House. How about another story like it but instead of Sonoma, set it right here in one of the American Colonies--maybe outside

ACT ONE; SCENE TWO

Tampico or South. The hero would be a U.S. Army Captain--a General's son who leads a company of irregulars to rescue the besieged colony. Laura, the heroine has a brother, a bit of a wild man, who's riding with Villa and that's why the Federales are coming-- to take it out on her...Blood lust...

[Jack reaches around, urging her to lie down beside him.]

JACK: If I started now I could have it out by Fall.

CHARMIAN: It's a ripping idea, Jack. Your books are always better when they have a good romance.

JACK: Like the one between man-mate and she-mate.

CHARMIAN: Oh, I think that would be a bit lusty for Jack London's reading public.

JACK: You do, eh?

[He unbuttons her blouse.]

CHARMIAN: Indeed...What about the captain's launch...We're already late man-mate...

[They kiss.]

JACK: We'll hire our own.

CHARMIAN: Make a grand entrance.

JACK: Be piped aboard...

BLACK OUT

VERACRUZ

ACT ONE; SCENE THREE
THE PORTALES--EVENING

The drinks are flowing. Jack's table includes Charmian, Dick Davis, and two other reporters whose backs are to the audience. Charmian, the center of attention, regales the men. Jack's irritation builds.

CHARMIAN: Jack and I will never go to another one of Admiral Fletcher's white parties. It was like, well, being in a steam bath in a full dress, petticoat, and corset.

DICK: We had a fine time, lunch at Bacci's, where Jimmy got blotto on some of the native brew and had to be sent home in a buggy, then the rest of us went to the bullfights. You should have been there Jack--

[Before Jack can respond.]

CHARMIAN: Jack and I would have loved to, but Jack wanted to interview the Admiral--so while he drank Bacardi lemonades under the bridge awning with Admiral Fletcher and his staff, I was assigned to play croquet on the forward deck of the USS Chester with a herd of perspiring Junior Officers.

DICK: Personally, I detest the game.

CHARMIAN: Ye Gods, a dog has more brains than to chase his ball in this weather. Jack said after we got ashore that----

JACK *[Interrupting]:* What's the complaint, you didn't have to come.

CHARMIAN: Oh, I think the Admiral would have been affronted--

JACK: Fletcher didn't even know you were in Veracruz. Whadya say Gents? Why don't we round up a donkey cart. Take a ride along the Malecón.

[Charmian loops her arm through Jack's.]

CHARMIAN: Mate, we have such a big day tomorrow. We're

ACT ONE; SCENE THREE

going to civil court in the morning.

[To the others]

We've heard it is just a sketch. There's this big ensign Olaf Sighanson, all 6' 4" inches of him presiding over these terrified little Mexicans brought in for public drunkenness and whatnot, who come up with the most outlandish excuses. We're bringing Reuterdahl to do the drawings.

[Jack reaches for the rum bottle. Charmian moves it out of his reach. Jack motions to Dick to pass it to him. Dick obliges.]

CHARMIAN: Then in the afternoon, we're going out with a Marine detachment to meet a refugee train. I think, mate, we had better--

JACK *[Ignoring her]*: Well, gents how 'bout that buggy ride? We'll stop in at Sor Juana's and enjoy a good cigar?

[Jack pours himself a large slug, fixing Charmian with a challenging glare. Charmian's jaw tightens, letting go of Jack.]

CHARMIAN: You don't think I know what Sor Juana's is, Jack?

JACK: A good Cigar, no harm in that? At least for those of us with ball and chain attached, eh?

[Jack laughs, Dick looks embarrassed.]

CHARMIAN: If you don't want me here with you Jack, I have no reason to stay.

JACK: Sure I want you here; but don't watch me like a damn hawk.

[The table goes absolutely silent. Charmian, furious, gets up, collecting her things. Jack tries to brush it over.]

JACK: Just giving you some straight-fisted talk, mate, no harm meant.

CHARMIAN: If you will excuse me, Gentlemen.

[Charmian exits. Jack half-rises to go after her then lets her go. Others grab for their drinks, embarrassed.]

JACK: She'll buck up. How about it boys?, Shall we pay our respects to Sor Juana?

DICK: If I were you, Jack m'boy--

JACK *[Challenging]:* But you aren't, Dickie.

DICK *[Shrugs]:* Well, you're on your own. I'm done in.

The other reporters nod in agreement.

JACK: What do I have here?--I thought hardy red-blooded adventuresome men --but now I find, a bunch of weak-livered nells.

[The other reporters wave good-night as they exit.]

DICK: Jack, there you are, the end of the evening and the last man standing. It will be the death of you.

JACK: Life is the death of us all. I have no intention of wasting my days trying to prolong them.

DICK: "Wasting my days trying to prolong them."

Good, Jack--I think I'll steal it.

JACK: Yours for the taking, Dick.

DICK: Good-night, Jack.

JACK: What? My words for the taking but you won't stay with me for an evening of adventure?

[Jack shouts at Dick as he exits into the hotel.]

JACK: The hell with you, then, and I'll take my words back!

DICK: Night, Jack.

[Jack leans back in his chair. He signals to the Musicians off-stage. We hear the distinctive Veracruz Jarocho music.

Douglas enters. He is dressed formally in a custom-tailored tropical uniform. Douglas spots Jack and walks over. Jack looks up, bleary eyed, not placing him at first.]

ACT ONE; SCENE THREE

DOUGLAS: Jack, I was on my way to leave a message for you at the desk. I was afraid I had missed you. The general's dinner was interminable.

JACK: Oh right, Doug, the General's son.

DOUGLAS: Douglas, Jack.

JACK: Sit down, lad, take a load off.

[To a waiter]

Compañero!

[The waiter brings an empty glass for Douglas and Jack fills it from his bottle.]

DOUGLAS: Thank you. Fascinating, Veracruz, it all starts from here. Cortes, Maximillian, Winfield Scott in '48.

JACK: Your father fight with Scott?

DOUGLAS: Lord no. The Governor was only eighteen when the Civil War began--Missionary Ridge was where he made his mark.

JACK: Now, there's a story! The charge up Missionary Ridge that opened the South to the Union Army. And now you'll lead Funston's charge to the capital.

DOUGLAS: An expeditionary force would be commanded by a four-star general.

JACK: That would be your mentor. So it will be "To the Heights" with General Wood?

[A wink]

With Captain MacArthur at his side?

[He tops off Douglas' glass and refills his own.]

DOUGLAS: I wish I knew, Jack. The Socialists are not the only problem. It remains to be seen whether President Wilson has the stomach for it.

JACK: I would not have guessed it. He looks to all the world like stern stuff.

VERACRUZ

DOUGLAS: Don't repeat this and for God's sake if you do, don't say where you heard it, but the President's steward said he had to wash out his underwear after Garrison told him there were eighteen sailors dead in Veracruz.

JACK: I'll be damned. The inside story on the President's knickers. I don't think Colliers wants that one, Doug, but front and center on General Wood's march to Mexico City, both I and my publisher would be in your debt. Where does the cabinet stand on the invasion?

DOUGLAS: Secretary Garrison, General Wood, and Colonel House have been hammering away at the President to commit but Bryan keeps reminding him that eighteen dead is more than Dewey suffered when he took the Philippines. He's pushing the President to arbitrate.

JACK: A stalemate, eh--I guess it's home to the ranch.

DOUGLAS: Unless we can convince President Wilson that we can take Mexico City and take it fast enough so that by the time the casualty reports reach home we have the flag flying over the Castle of Chapultepec.

JACK: You were in on the discussions?

DOUGLAS: Privy to them--until I was dispatched.

JACK: To devise a plan to take the capital?

DOUGLAS: You did not hear me say that, Mr. London.

JACK *[Intense]:* Said or not that's the logic of your words. Doug, I'm a reporter but you tell me something in confidence, man-to-man--it remains a confidence--Colliers be damned.

DOUGLAS: I sense that you are a man of your word and I'll take you at it. We need locomotives, Jack, that's the only way we are going to get a force to Mexico City quick enough. And there are none to be had. The Mexicans knew what they were doing when they pulled all of theirs out of Veracruz. We

ACT ONE; SCENE THREE

need two strong pullers that can haul one hundred and fifty cars filled with troops and supplies and we need them soon or Bryan will have his arbitration. Already some of Wilson's East Coast banking friends are turning cautious.

JACK: Damn, I know what you're planning! Grab the refugee trains when they come.

DOUGLAS: That was the Marines' plan. Smedley Butler's overly frank estimate of a thousand casualties to secure the railhead at Puebla and two thousand more to take the capital doomed the plan. Wilson rejected it out-of-hand, which was just as well as it would have put the Navy back in the lead. I need a plan that doesn't have those casualty figures attached.

JACK: After Colonel Roosevelt and San Juan Hill, it'll be Captain MacArthur at the Halls of Montezuma! And I'll write it: good hard action.

DOUGLAS: In the tradition of Homer.

JACK: I didn't hear you say your Goddamns were packing the Iliad in their rucksacks, Doug. I wager you're headed for your first General's star.

[Flattered, Douglas laughs and refills Jack's glass.]

DOUGLAS: With Jack London telling my story, perhaps so.

[Jack toasts Douglas.]

JACK: One thing I know how to write and that's a ripping adventure.

DOUGLAS: Jack, you make no bones about it, you see into the heart of the matter and you let people know what it is you see. The Governor, that's what my brother and I called our father, always advised us that if you want to take the true measure of a man consider him not on his horse with medals on his chest, but as his tailor would--in his underwear.

VERACRUZ

JACK: I would like to have shared my fire with your father.

DOUGLAS: He would have liked you, Jack--straight off. Tell me about your father, or should I have heard of him?

JACK *[Bitter sadness]:* Heard of him, Doug, I shouldn't think so, I barely have. By all accounts I'm a bastard. My mother claims I was fathered by a William Chaney, an itinerant clairvoyant, astrologer, patent medicine salesman and President of The Chicago College of Astrology and Kindred Sciences, which he also founded, and is its one and only faculty member.

DOUGLAS: Jack I--

JACK: Perhaps he was her Mack. You know what a Mack is, Doug?

DOUGLAS: O, I don't--

[Jack waves him off.]

JACK: I wrote him after I published Call of the Wild and it had reached its thirteenth printing to general acclaim, introducing myself, his son. He wrote back saying that he was impotent when my mother and he cohabited. He further added that my mother had many gentlemen callers.

DOUGLAS *[Uptight]:* Jack, please, I didn't--

JACK: Well, there you have the story of my breeding, Doug. Sometimes the truth gives you a bloody nose.

[Jack signals the musicians and they begin another tune.]

DOUGLAS: But look what you made of yourself, Jack. You are a tribute to the Anglo-Saxon race.

JACK: Neither dog nor man can rise above his breeding.

DOUGLAS: I for one am honored to have spent an evening with the most famous author in America.

JACK: And it's not over yet, my friend

[Signaling off stage]

ACT ONE; SCENE THREE

Compañero!

[O.S. Sound of a horse-drawn carriage.]

JACK: How about a turn around the Malecón during the only time of the day in Veracruz when a man doesn't feel he's taking the updraft of a furnace into his lungs and then we'll stop in at Sor Juana's.

DOUGLAS: Is that one of the places that Funston set up for the men?

JACK: God, no. Those are drenched in the reproving smell of carbolic acid. Sor Juana's is a bit unauthorized. It has the soft scent of sin about it.

DOUGLAS: It wouldn't be good at all to be found in a place like that. I think I best turn in. Captain Burnside has arranged a long day--

JACK *[Seductive]:* Doug, the night is young, we'll stop for a nightcap and a good cigar.

DOUGLAS *[Flustered]:* Those places just aren't for me. Mother made my brother and me promise that we would avoid just such places as your Sor Juana's.

JACK *[Sharp]:* Some hard-fisted truth, Doug, get off the tit.

DOUGLAS: Now hold on--

JACK: Don't take offense, Doug,

DOUGLAS: It's Douglas, Jack, how many times do I have to tell you?

JACK: To your mother, bless her soul, Doug. But with me it's man to man. I say it again, Doug, get off the tit.

DOUGLAS: I think we had better end this discussion, Mr. London, right now!

JACK: I know you want to go, Doug, and you know that I know--and what red-blooded man wouldn't? Come on, I won't peach.

VERACRUZ

[For a moment we think Doug might punch Jack, then Doug reconsiders.]

DOUGLAS: Too close to home. Perhaps you're right. I was mocked at the Academy when it became known that mother had taken rooms at Craney's across the street from the campus.

JACK: Can you smell it on the wind--the jacaranda beckoning...

DOUGLAS: Invited out on the town, by Jack London, the famous American author, now how bad can that be?

[Jack offers Doug his arm. They exit.]

BLACK OUT

ACT 0NE; SCENE FOUR
SOR JUANA'S

Piano Music; soft and jazzy. Lushly decadent, Sor Juana's bordello spreads across the stage in rich velvet reds.

Stage left is a bar and a billiard table that disappears offstage.

Jack and Douglas enter stage right. They join another man on the divans.

DOUGLAS: Jack, I think this is ill-advised.

JACK: Doug, your third leg's as hard as mine.

DOUGLAS: It's Douglas and--

JACK: Women here are to be had and nothing wrong with it. It's a fair and honorable exchange. A free-thinking woman chooses to make twenty dollars a night lying on her back, a man on top of her, over a life of toil in some God-forsaken sweatshop where more than likely she is raped by boss, foreman or both. Either way she has a man on top of her and who among us has the right to fault her for choosing the profitable alternative. If I was born of the female sex you can bet I'd have my application in at Sor Juana's.

BILL: Well said, Mr. London, well said. Bill Buckley.

[Bill Buckley grips Jack's hand with one hand and his elbow with the other, his signature greeting. Buckley is a handsome Texan, with a pleasant, folksy manner. He wears a light linen guayaberra--dressed comfortably for the weather.]

JACK: Always a pleasure to meet a man who sees my point. If I'm not mistaken you're the oil lawyer who sits on the Council of the Occupation?

BILL: I'm afraid I stand rightly accused. And you, Captain, nice to see you again. We were introduced tonight--at the General's party.

DOUGLAS: I'm sorry, but--

BILL: You must have been introduced to half of Veracruz. Captain Burnside told me he has arranged for us to lunch tomorrow.

DOUGLAS *[Embarrassed]:* Oh yes, I look forward to it. We were just stopping here for a drink.

BILL: Oh, you'll be missing a great deal, Captain, if alcohol is all that touches your lips at Sor Juana's.

[Jack laughs. Douglas blushes but nevertheless is put at his ease. China Girl, a childlike whore, in a skimpy Chinese dress, enters and sits at the bar, attracting Doug's attention. Bill signals off-stage to a buxom redhead and gets up.]

BILL: I'll see you boys later.

[Bill exits as Sor Juana enters. She is dressed in a cream-colored man's suit of Egyptian linen.]

SOR JUANA: Jackie, so happy that we see you. I thought you had forsaken me.

[They kiss on both cheeks.]

JACK: Sor Juana, you know my heart belongs to you.

SOR JUANA: I think it is not your heart, Jackie.

[With a wink, Sor Juana turns her big saucer eyes full bore on Douglas.]

SOR JUANA: Who is your handsome Yankee Captain?

[But Jack is entranced with Rosa, also off-stage. Sor Juana smiles.]

SOR JUANA: Jackie? Do you have a special caballita picked out?

JACK *[Grabbing her, playful]:* You bet your bottom.

ACT ONE; SCENE FOUR

[Sor Juana playfully slaps Jack's cheek.]

SOR JUANA: A caballita you could ride. Be a good boy and make my acquaintance with your handsome captain.

JACK: Doug, Sor Juana. And if you can bed her you're a better man than I.

[Jack, with a wink to Douglas, gets up and, exits through the curtains.]

SOR JUANA: Captain, Jackie is such a wicked, faithless boy--I'm afraid he wants another. And to think I saved my maidenhead for him.

[Slow on the uptake, finally, Douglas laughs. Sor Juana follows Douglas's gaze and signals China Girl to join them.]

SOR JUANA: But you are more refined, subtle. Fascinated by the mysteries of the East. I hope you are a strong man, my dear captain, because our China Girl has a sad story.

[China Girl walks over, eyes modestly downcast. Her Mayan features are covered with porcelain white pancake makeup. Sor Juana guides her into the seat Jack has vacated.]

SOR JUANA: China Girl is for you, Captain.

DOUGLAS: Oh no, I don't think that will be necessary I--

SOR JUANA: A favor to me, Captain. China Girl is new here and needs to be treated gently.

[Sor Juana whispers something to China Girl. She moves closes to Doug, touching him.]

CHINA GIRL: My Captain, I first ask you what you want to drink?

DOUGLAS: Yes, well, how kind. What is it you have?

CHINA GIRL: Champagne.

DOUGLAS: There. Good. Champagne it is, then.

[Sor Juana brings the champagne and two glasses. China

Girl pours. Caressing Doug's hand when she passes the glass.]

DOUGLAS: I don't want you to have the wrong impression. I am here inadvertently.

SOR JUANA: Yes, my Captain, so is the China Girl; but she is here with you.

[China Girl takes Douglas' hands. Turning the right one palm up, she traces his lifeline.]

CHINA GIRL: You have good hands my Captain. Now I will tell your fortune.

DOUGLAS: There is no need.

SOR JUANA: The Captain would like China Girl to please him in other ways?

[China Girl presses against Doug, turning him on.]

DOUGLAS: Sor Juana, you must tell me about China Girl, yes, you must tell me her story.

[Sor Juana motions to the piano player off-stage. A tin pan alley faux Chinese melody plays.

As Sor Juana sings The Song of the China Girl, China girl continues her seduction.]

SOR JUANA *[lyrics & music Bruce Barthol]:*

PRETTY CHINA GIRL FROM CHANG CHING WEE
ONLY DAUGHTER OF SHIP CHANDLER MING LEE
HE WAS HIGHLY RESPECTED BY EVERY SHIP AND SKIPPER
FROM THE KOWLOON JUNK TO THE YANKEE CLIPPER.
BUT MING LEE HAD A WEAKNESS, A SECRET YEN
FOR THE PIPE AND THE FLOWER OF THE OPIUM DEN
LITTLE BY LITTLE AND DAY BY DAY
MING LEE SMOKED HIS FORTUNES AWAY. HE SMOKED
TILL HIS BUSINESS AND HIS HOME WERE GONE

ACT ONE; SCENE FOUR

WITH NOTHING LEFT TO SELL OR PAWN
THEN A YANKEE CAPTAIN WHO HAD SEEN THE CHINA GIRL
OFFERED TO BUY HER FOR A BAG OF PEARLS.
POOR MING LEE HE CRIED AND WAILED
BUT HE TOOK THE PEARLS AND MADE THE SALE
POOR MING HE LACKED THE POWER
TO RESIST THE LURE OF THE OPIUM FLOWER. AND
WHAT DOES MING LEE HEAR CHINA GIRL SAY
AS SHE STANDS ON THE DECK AND SAILS AWAY?
SHE SAY:

[China girl caresses Doug's thigh; he puts his arm around her.]

CHINA GIRL:

ME NO LIKEE CHINAMAN
ME LIKEE TALL AND BLUE-EYED AMERICAN
ME LIKEE GO ACROSS THE SEA
AWAY FROM MING LEE AND CHANG CHING WEE.
ME KNOWEE SECRETS OF THE ORIENT
SHOWEE TO MY MAN FROM THE OCCIDENT
ME LIKEE HAVE AMERICAN PAPPY

CHINA GIRL & SOR JUANA:

MAKE HER HAPPY, MAKE HIM HAPPY
MAKE ME HAPPY, MAKE YOU HAPPY

[China Girl takes Douglas's hand and puts it on her breast.]

DOUGLAS: Oh my poor little China Girl, your Captain will protect you.

CHINA GIRL: Now you will come to my room and comfort me.

DOUGLAS: Yes, yes, China Girl, I will do my best.

END OF ACT

VERACRUZ

ACT TWO; SCENE ONE
SOR JUANA'S LATER

Bill Buckley idly plays billiards by himself. Off-stage we hear the balls click against each other.

Jack swaggers in and stands, his back to the bar, watching Buckley.

JACK: What a ride! That Rosa has more ups and downs than a steeplechase.

[*Bill laughs.*]

BILL: I'll have to pay her a visit.

[*Jack picks up a cue-stick and takes a turn. As he shoots.*]

JACK: Damn, I'm hungry. What I'd do for some abalone.

BILL: They have oysters.

JACK: Oysters? You dare compare the saintly abalone to the lowly slimy smelly stinking oyster! Abalone is a clean piece of white steak, fresh, tender and tasty as your sweetheart's cheek.

[*Jack whistles a bar THEN SINGS*]

"OH! SOME FOLKS BOAST OF QUAIL ON TOAST
BECAUSE THEY THINK IT'S TONEY
BUT I'M CONTENT TO OWE MY RENT
AND LIVE ON ABALONE!"

What I'd give to be back on the beach in Carmel with 'the crowd' around a big bonfire, The Greek putting the steaks on sticks--that's the best way, really, cut straight out of the shell, live, singing in the fire with a squeeze of lemon juice on them...Lord oh Lord

[*singing*]

"OH SOME LIKE JAM, AND SOME LIKE HAM

ACT TWO; SCENE ONE

AND SOME LIKE MACARONI;
BUT BRING ME IN A PAIL OF GIN
AND A TUB OF ABALONE."

[Sor Juana enters with a tray of tapas.]

JACK *[To Sor Juana and Bill]*: Come on, give me the chorus.
"OH! SOME FOLKS BOAST OF QUAIL ON TOAST
BECAUSE THEY THINK IT'S TONEY."

[They join in, accompanied by the piano off-stage. Jack, the choirmaster, conducts with a cue stick.]

BILL & SOR JUANA

"OH! SOME FOLKS BOAST OF QUAIL ON TOAST
BECAUSE THEY THINK IT'S TONEY... BUT I'M CONTENT
TO OWE MY RENT
AND LIVE ON ABALONE."

JACK: Bravo!

[Delighted, Jack lays down his cue stick and helps himself to Sor Juana's tapas.]

JACK: Sor Juana, you can come to my ranch anytime long as you bring a sack of these chilies.

SOR JUANA: Then I could meet Señora London?

JACK: Hell yes, why not. She's met people in far more disreputable professions. In New York we had dinner with Mr. Hearst.

[Buckley laughs. Jack chows down on some chili peppers.]

JACK: You know what would be good with these?

BILL: Don't tell me.

JACK: But I will. These chilies wrapped in a big raw abalone steak.

BILL: Looking at them makes my `you-know-what' burn.

[Jack puts two in his mouth for emphasis.]

VERACRUZ

JACK: A Chili doesn't deserve the name if it doesn't make you want to sit on a block of ice next morning.

[Jack sucks down the rest of his beer and settles in, nursing his copa.]

JACK: What did you do with my Captain, Sor Juana?

SOR JUANA: Your Captain fell in love with my China Girl.

JACK: That I can't understand. No tits, no ass.

BILL: Some day maybe I'll sample the mysteries of the Orient.

JACK: You come to San Francisco and I'll take you to Mother Lee's.

BILL: Damned if I don't.

JACK: If I don't miss my guess a man like you must know this country pretty well?

BILL: As much as anybody can know it. It isn't easy getting your hands around it. I've been down here since the Tampico strike. Those were the days, put a stick in the ground, oil come out. But when Diaz skedaddled, everything went to hell.

JACK: So as it stands now it's all a loss.

BILL: Up in Tampico, where I've been based, it's been full-time trying to keep it from being blown up. You pay off a Federale General then a Constitutionalist comes along wanting the same or more. Then you got to pay them both again to get them to keep Villa's boys off your back. But it's a rich country, Jack, too rich for us to turn our backs on and it can be summed up in one word: OIL!

Navies all over the world, converting their fleets to it. One ton of it does the work of six ton of coal. The Twentieth Century is oil! And as far as people can figure out a good percentage of the world's supply is within a hundred miles of where we're standing. But somebody has got to convince

ACT TWO; SCENE ONE

Brother Woodrow to grab these Mexicans by the scruff of the neck and shake some sense into their heads so we can get at it. We don't do something soon they'll ruin their whole damn country.

JACK: I could agree they need a strong leader but one from the masses-- Another Diaz if you will, but with the interests of the Mexican people in his heart.

BILL: Sounds like socialist poppycock--no offense.

JACK: "The meek shall inherit the earth." Jesus Christ.

BILL: But, in His infinite wisdom, He didn't say anything about mineral rights.

JACK *[Laughs]:* You're a corker, Bill--I like the cut of your mizzen, my friend.

BILL: Like-wise, Jack.

JACK: Bill, I've been planning to do a feature on our settlers down here. Not just the ones you meet on the refugee trains but the big boys, the empire builders. Perhaps you could introduce me around?

BILL: I'd be honored. I'm going up to Tampico day after tomorrow for five or six days. Why don't you come with me. We'll go out to one of Harry Chandler's spreads. He's got 200,000 acres a few miles north of the town. The proviso being we can stick our heads up without getting shot at.

JACK: The timing couldn't be better; I'm sure my wife would agree.

BILL: I'll send a car for you and Mrs. London.

JACK: I'll be on my lonesome, Bill, Mrs. London is not in the mood to travel--not in my company.

[Fred Boalt enters with Ensign William "Bully" Richardson, 21, close at his side. Tall, bronzed, confident as befitting "the best fullback Annapolis ever had."]

VERACRUZ

FRED: There he is. Jack!

JACK *[singing]:*
"ARISE YE PRISONERS OF STARVATION!
ARISE YE--"

FRED *[Interrupting]:* Jack. Jack. A young man off the Arkansas wants to meet you.

[Fred urges Bully forward. Jack offers Bully his hand.]

BULLY: Bully Richardson, sir, I'm so honored to meet you. I must have read your Call of the Wild twenty times.

JACK: Twenty times? That could well be a record, Bully.

BULLY: I named my own dog Buck, Mr. London.

JACK: My friends call me Jack--or worse. I don't have Call with me, but we have advance copies of my newest-Strength of the Strong. I'll leave an autographed copy for you at the Diligencias.

BULLY: Thank you, Sir--Jack.

JACK *[Taking out a dog-eared notebook]:* "Sir Jack" whadya know--knighted in a whorehouse--Write how you want your name.

[Fred takes advantage of the opening as Bully writes in Jack's notebook.]

FRED: Jack, Bully was in the thick of it on the twenty-first and twenty-second.

JACK: You don't say. See plenty of action?

FRED: Bully commanded one of the squads that took fire at the Naval Academy.

BULLY: After our lieutenant was wounded.

JACK: Lost a lot of men there, I heard.

BULLY: We weren't expecting it--I guess you know. Said we could just plan on walking in like we were on parade. Boy, did they have that wrong. If it wasn't for The Chester's guns, the greasers would've killed us all.

ACT TWO; SCENE ONE

JACK: How many men did you lose, Bully?

BULLY: Four men and I don't mind telling you it still makes my blood boil to think of it. Just pure meanness really. The Mexes knew they couldn't stop us taking the city, so they just made sport like we were fish in a barrel.

FRED: Bully, tell Jack about the one on the balcony.

BULLY: If that didn't beat all. Before we got to the Naval Academy along Francisco Canal that runs right into the plaza--Bang! Our Bosun, Jonesy, goes down. I pull our squad back behind the corner. Jonesy's out there in the street- I mean like it was a fountain coming out of him and him squirming around, screaming, dragging his legs behind like a dog with a broken back. "Come and get me boys, come and get me!" Seaman Lane goes out to pull in Jonesy but he got shot in the face, so I go out and pull Jonesy in but he's already dead by then and we're holed up there trying to spot the sniper, when a squad from the New Hampshire comes into the intersection from the other direction. Their point man got it right in the chest. Then I spotted him; this old greaser, dressed in his Sunday best, sitting on his balcony with his newspaper in his lap. But he wasn't reading it, no sir, underneath it he had his little pistol that he was using to pot-shot us pretty as you please. Our rifleman took him out, one shot to the head.

JACK: He must have known he'd be spotted sooner or later.

BULLY: That's the way they fight, underhanded, like they aren't really doing it--When we took them prisoner it was the same from all of them. "No, no señor eese not mee, eet is mi brother, señor he eese shooting I promise you before zee holy blessed virgin." Lying bastards! Every last one of them!

JACK: That's quite a story, Bully. I'm down here on assignment

VERACRUZ

for Colliers Weekly and I'd like to write it up.

[Jack pulls out a pocket notebook and pen.]

JACK: Folks at home sure want to read about it. Kind of Fred to steer you to me...You said your squad was off the U.S.S. Arkansas?

[Douglas enters through the curtains, unnoticed.]

FRED: Wait, Jack, you haven't heard all of it. Bully's squad was put in charge of guarding the suspected snipers that were taken prisoner.

JACK: Tell me about it, Bully.

BULLY: We had them in a warehouse just off the Malecón. They thought we were going to shoot them. That's what they do with their prisoners; it's up against the wall and no bones about it. We decided to give them a sporting chance. I had my men let them out two at a time. We gave them a half block lead before we opened up on them. If they made it to the corner, fine--if they didn't--well it was a better chance than they would have given us.

BILL: They call it the ley de fuega. Down here it's the squarest deal you get.

BULLY: I showed them the iron hand--something they understand.

JACK *[Shocked]*: Any get away?

BULLY: A couple, when the gun jammed. I don't mind telling you, those were a pair of happy greasers.

[Douglas inserts himself.]

DOUGLAS: Douglas MacArthur, ensign, pleasure to meet you.

BULLY: Ensign William Richardson, sir.

JACK: Doug, you hear what this lad was telling us?

DOUGLAS: A bit of it, Jack, I was just making Ensign Richardson's acquaintance.

[Douglas turns back to Bully, interposing himself between

ACT TWO; SCENE ONE

Bully and Jack and Fred.
Jack orders another drink from the bar as Doug presses in on Bully. Fred watches with growing alarm.]

DOUGLAS: Not the Bully Richardson. Not the Navy fullback Richardson who thrashed us good and hard in last year's game at The Point?

BULLY: I'm afraid I must admit to it.

DOUGLAS: That was some thrashing you gave us. I remember that last run you made, forty-six yards, threw off three of our best men. Dashed our hopes that day, Bully.

BULLY: I can't say we didn't have a little luck going with us.

[Douglas pushes up close and personal.]

DOUGLAS: Not luck, you played a fine game, Ensign. Tops. Too bad you were on the other team. Now, Mr. London is a fine fellow, the other reporter too.

BULLY: I'm a great admirer of Mr. London. I was telling him I read Call of--

DOUGLAS: Mr. London isn't here writing dog stories, he's a reporter, writing up stories like the one you've just told for Americans at home to read.

BULLY: He told me he's writing for Colliers. My mom and dad take--

DOUGLAS: Americans don't want to read some foolish bragging by American soldiers claiming they were shooting prisoners.

BULLY: But.

DOUGLAS: Ensign Richardson, how would you like to spend the rest of your life in a navy brig for shooting prisoners of war?

FRED: Hey, what the hell, you're trying to shut him up!

BULLY: I--uh.

DOUGLAS: Son, get back to your ship.

VERACRUZ

FRED: What the hell! Let him tell his story. How many Mexes you shoot, Bully?

[Douglas keeps Bully in his unrelenting stare. With an angry glance at Fred, Bully exits.]

FRED *[Outraged]:* You saw that, Jack.

[Douglas turns, gracing Fred with a conciliatory smile.]

DOUGLAS: Not a word of truth in it. Just soldiers' talk, you hear it after every engagement--what they thought they should do, wanted to do, or heard was done. Perhaps a sniper or two was dealt with peremptorily but nothing more.

FRED: He shot prisoners. Self-confessed. You heard him. The iron hand is what he called it. It's against the rules of civilized warfare.

DOUGLAS: And I'm telling you, sir, there is nothing to it except youthful bragging about something that never happened. You know if I had to hazard a guess my bet is that the ensign missed the action. Killing a man, putting an end to a life, well, those who have done it don't brag about it. Am I right, Jack?

JACK: That young man told a hard tale.

DOUGLAS: I know the quality of our soldiers and they do not shoot prisoners even under the most extreme circumstances and I defy you to prove otherwise.

FRED: But I don't have to prove it. We all just heard Ensign Bully Richardson confess it. Right, Jack?

[Jack starts to speak but Douglas cuts him off.]

DOUGLAS: I say we heard a lad with an unblemished record. A sporting hero. A picture portrait of American Anglo-Saxon manhood, drunk in a whorehouse, tell a tall tale to a couple of civilians about something he never did.

JACK: Why'd you chase him? I would have thought you'd want to challenge him. Correct the story then and there.

ACT TWO; SCENE ONE

DOUGLAS: Jack, this fellow, what is your name, sir?

FRED: Fred Boalt, Newspaper Enterprise Association.

DOUGLAS: Because, Mr. Boalt would have been on him all night and he would have dug himself a pretty hole. I know how it is with most members of the press. General MacArthur was often libeled by them. In the Philippines they disparaged him at every opportunity until the President felt obliged to relieve him.

JACK: Your father aside Doug, it seems to me that ensign's story bares looking into.

DOUGLAS: Jack, you're a man of some experience. When did you last give credence to anything said in a whorehouse?

JACK: Fred, you have to admit he has a point. That's what men do in whorehouses: boast about chesty adventures they never had.

FRED *[Confused]:* Jack, you heard him! He wasn't bragging, it was more like he was telling you something that was right to have done. He didn't see anything wrong with it.

JACK: Fred, for the sake of argument consider Doug's point. A young man sees his friends die--not a manly death like Sir Lancelot, King Arthur, and, yes, like my books. He sees them die by trickery. Die, Fred! His bosun squirting blood in the street. Watches another seaman's face disintegrate to bone and blood! After it's over the young man, nay, boy, imagines how he should have taken his revenge. It is well-conceived and moralistic and it is told in the language his tormentors could understand. But as far as we know, it is only a tale of what a young soldier would have liked to have done or perhaps heard someone else do.

FRED: I've been a reporter long enough to know when a man is telling a tall tale and when he's not! Ensign Bully Richardson recounted a cold-blooded murder of prisoners of war, pure and simple. I heard talk about you, Jack, but I never believed it.

JACK: What talk?

FRED: With your ranch and success and all, there are some that wonder what side you are on.

JACK: Truth. I'm on the side of truth, Fred. You need something more than whorehouse talk to give credence to that tale before Jack London or any other fair minded journalist would put his name to it.

FRED: When I do I expect you to stand beside me and The Cause.

JACK: Not you, Fred, nor what you in your twenty some years of wisdom pronounce as The Cause. Truth is what I stand beside. You bring me truth. Bring some other evidence besides the bragging of a twenty year old lad with a head full of drink and I will stand by it.

FRED: Comrade London, you can count on it.

[Boalt storms out. Jack grabs another drink, upset.]

BILL: The Newspaper that gent writes for. Never heard of it?

JACK: Some of the boys put it together. They syndicate to the dailies. They have a room and a ticker back in Chicago.

BILL: Pinko outfit, huh?

JACK: Pinko? If by that you mean that they are sympathetic to the rights of the American working man, yes they are and I'm proud to have been syndicated by them.

BILL: No offense, Jack, we're all Americans here.

[Changing the subject]

Captain, it must be quite exciting to be on the General Staff and, from what I hear, General Wood's top aide?

DOUGLAS: It's an honor to serve under General Wood.

ACT TWO; SCENE ONE

BILL: If only he was running things down here instead of the politicians. Through my dear friend Colonel House, I'm well aware of General Wood's views regarding Mexico.

DOUGLAS: You know the Colonel?

BILL: We're next door neighbors in Austin. The Colonel telegraphed that I should be on the lookout for you--he mentioned that there was a question of adequate transportation for an expeditionary force.

DOUGLAS: Yes, but I'm surprised that--

BILL *[Confidentially]:* I took the liberty of making some inquiries. There are two Baldwin locomotives parked on a siding at the Sanborn coffee plantation forty miles south at the junction of the Alvarado line.

DOUGLAS *[Thrilled!]:* Baldwins? You couldn't want any better.

BILL: That's my information. They're owned by a German bank but I can make arrangements for their lease.

DOUGLAS: I'll need them inspected. Make sure they are in working order.

BILL: I've been assured that they are but if you want to have a look yourself, I could arrange it. Overland is through Zapatista territory but the plantation is quite accessible by launch from the coast. You just let me know and I'll have you down there in a couple hours time.

DOUGLAS: With two Baldwins, everything is in place.

[A commotion stage right. Sor Juana enters, furious, with a disheveled and bruised China Girl beside her. She pushes China Girl toward Jack.]

SOR JUANA: Jackie, look what your Captain has done to my China Girl.

DOUGLAS: There is some mistake. I did nothing--

[China Girl lunges at Douglas but Sor Juana grabs her.]

VERACRUZ

CHINA GIRL: Maricón!

DOUGLAS *[Self righteous]:* This is absurd, Gentlemen. I don't know why this--

[China Girl breaks free of Sor Juana's grip and drawing a knife, goes for Douglas.]

CHINA GIRL: Yanqui Pendejo!

[Jack tries to intercept China Girl but he's too slow. Douglas neatly executes a basic judo move, grabbing her at the wrist and twists hard. China Girl screams, dropping the knife. Douglas lets her go. She falls back cradling her injured arm in the other.]

DOUGLAS: I know what's going on here. This little tart--yes I heard about it in the Philippines. She is attempting to extort money. I think they called them putas--

[China Girl spits in Douglas' face. He slaps her knocking her down.]

SOR JUANA: This is going to make trouble for us all.

[Bill steps between Douglas and Sor Juana.

BILL: Sor Juana, my deepest apologies

[Jack takes Douglas by the arm.]

JACK: Time to leave, Doug.

DOUGLAS: I have been insulted.

BILL: Captain, Mr. London is giving you some good advice.

[Douglas allows himself to be led away. They exit. Bill turns back to Sor Juana.]

BILL: Sor Juana, the Captain meant no harm.

SOR JUANA: No harm, you say? Look what this degenerado did. She won't be able to work for months.

[Sor Juana thrusts China Girl at Buckley to inspect.]

BILL: Allow me to make an adjustment.

[Bill removes some cash from his wallet and gives her

some, then some more. Finally satisfied, Sor Juana takes them and leads China Girl away, comforting her with the money. Music.]

BLACK OUT

VERACRUZ

ACT TWO; SCENE TWO
IN FRONT OF SOR JUANA'S--EVENING

Doug and Jack enter. Doug is agitated, nervous.

DOUGLAS: Jack, I assure you that I didn't force her to do anything--well--unnatural.

JACK: You could have got your throat slit.

DOUGLAS: If my death comes prematurely it will be on a battlefield. I swear if she had come at me again I would have put her down.

JACK: Some straight fisted advice. You want something special arrange it with the madam before you--

DOUGLAS *[Interrupting]:* But that was not the case. The tart tried to rob me and I caught her at it. I assure you as an officer and a gentleman that is what happened.

JACK: Buck up, Doug, it's over and done with.

DOUGLAS: Yes, of course but...

[Pause]

It wouldn't do at all if this was talked about--if there should be a complaint lodged. Perhaps some extra compensation is in order? A gesture of goodwill.

JACK: Bill's taking care of it.

DOUGLAS: Then enough said?

JACK: Mum's the word.

[Doug relaxes.]

DOUGLAS: You're a friend indeed, Jack.

JACK *[Hailing a carriage]:* Compañero!

[Horse hooves clatter on the cobblestones. The carriage's shadow falls across the stage. They let it wait.]

DOUGLAS: That fellow, you think he's going to write up that Ensign's tale?

ACT TWO; SCENE TWO

JACK: Hell yes! The lad thinks he's going to stop the war with it.

DOUGLAS: You and I know the reality of battle. But what about the citizens at home--the mothers and fathers? What if they were to read that their boys are shooting prisoners?

JACK: Boalt will write the story, nothing you can do about that unless you want to shoot him. I know, I was like that.

DOUGLAS *[From memory]:* "Who will take it from you? We will! And who are we? We are the seven million Socialist revolutionists and we are everywhere and growing." You're quite a firebrand. Captain Burnside showed me your file from the War Department.

JACK: What's it under, who to shoot when the revolution comes?

DOUGLAS: Hardly, Jack, they keep files on the opinions of our country's leading citizens for reference. Do you still stand by those words, Jack?

JACK: These days I struggle to keep my ranch going, help my friends and my alleged friends. But I still believe in the ideals of Socialism-- although I have given up hope that I will ever see it come to pass.

DOUGLAS: Do you believe in destiny, Jack?

JACK: The superstitious belief held by the rich to explain why they have everything and the poor nothing? Man is a product of his society, his class and his race. Destiny, predestination, whatever you call it, is a bunch of superstitious horseshit.

DOUGLAS: Then explain Rockefeller, the shopkeeper's son who becomes the wealthiest man in America. The centurion who becomes a Caesar? The slave's son who graduates with a doctorate from Harvard? And, yes, explain Jack London, who rises above his breeding and becomes the greatest writer in America.

VERACRUZ

JACK: Two words: Work. Determination.

DOUGLAS: There is something else and that's Destiny. The spirit force you won't give credence. It's why most brave boys died but my father never hesitated and thus lived to plant his regiment's banner on top of Missionary Ridge.

JACK: I'll admit to luck--that I'll grant you.

DOUGLAS: Luck comes and goes, Jack, but a man who acknowledges his destiny will have the strength to persevere and the courage to make the right choices because the Almighty will be at his side.

Our destiny brought us here to Mexico to protect those Anglo-Saxon pioneers of which you spoke so eloquently but even more to guide America on its march to leadership in this new Century. My destiny is to guide our nation on this perilous path and I say to you with utmost respect, I would be honored to have Jack London, the greatest writer in America, at my side.

JACK: Rest assured Doug, I'll be there!

[Jack grasps Doug's hand, Doug's response is tepid.]

DOUGLAS: I truly hope you will Jack but I'm concerned that you might be associated with Boalt's story.

JACK: If it gets picked up by the dailies, it will necessitate a comment. Everyone knows that I'm in Veracruz.

DOUGLAS: What if Boalt finds corroboration and asks you to add your byline?

JACK: Jack London has always stood by the truth.

DOUGLAS: There are many truths, Jack. One is that with those two Baldwin locomotives General Wood can guarantee President Wilson that he can have ten thousand troops patrolling the streets of Mexico City in 72 hours. Another truth is that a reporter who puts his name on an article reporting

ACT TWO; SCENE TWO

that Ensign's tale won't be with General Wood's Expeditionary Force but on the first transport leaving Veracruz.

[Douglas and Jack lock eyes.]

JACK *[Blustering]:* The Japs kicked me off the Russo-Japanese front for writing the truth--I never thought it would be done by a white man's army.

DOUGLAS: Jack, in this rarest of moments you will choose to either embrace your destiny and shoulder all the responsibility incumbent upon it or turn away. For your sake, for your nation's and your race I pray it is the former.

JACK: Now that's some straight-fisted talk, Doug, yes indeed.

[Doug fixes Jack with a steady gaze as he offers Jack his hand.]

BLACK OUT

VERACRUZ

ACT TWO; SCENE THREE
THE LONDON'S QUARTERS--FIVE DAYS LATER

Charmian sits at her writing table, typing. Jack bursts into the room, dusty from his trip to Tampico. His luggage, piled by the door, has preceded him. He goes to embrace her but she keeps her back to him. He delivers an awkward kiss to the side of her head.

JACK: Tampico, what a sight, Mate. Wish you had come. I saw ten thousand acres west of the Chandler spread-- good land, Charmian, and we could have it for less than a fourth of what we'd realize if we pulled up stakes and sold Beauty Ranch.

[He waits for her to look up. She doesn't. He extracts his spectacles from his pocket and reads over her shoulder.]

JACK: "The big brother can police, organize, and manage Mexico. Mexico's mongrel leadership cannot."--Let's change it to so-called leadership--Eh? "And the lives and happiness of a few million peons as well as the many millions yet to be born are at stake."

I'd say it's pretty damn good? And to hell with those damn ghetto socialists if they don't see the logic of it.

[Charmian turns and faces Jack.]

CHARMIAN: Logic? I'm afraid it escapes me as well. For a man who signs his letters, "Yours For The Revolution," I see no logic at all.

[Jack is momentarily taken aback, then seizes the opportunity to engage Charmian.]

JACK: Revolution when revolution means progress. In this poor country it stands for chaos. Charmian, hear me out, I've gained the confidence of Captain MacArthur, General

ACT TWO; SCENE THREE

Wood's chief aide. He's made the plans to take Mexico City. My guess is that they'll march as soon as General Wood arrives in Veracruz and I'll be right there with them. I have Captain MacArthur's word on it. This whole country is about to become a new American Frontier and I am here to tell the story of how America shoulders the responsibility of raising up a whole people out of a morass of self-destruction. Can't you see that?

CHARMIAN: Jack, I don't know any more who you are or what you've become. And I don't care.

[A pause. Jack reaches for her. She shakes him off.]

CHARMIAN: And I won't be treated like one of your whores or those little sycophants that follow you around like you were milk from their mother's tit!

JACK *[Stunned]:* Mate, you're giving me the Dickens and I deserve it. I said as much before I left for Tampico. I know I was cruel and disrespectful, but it was John Barleycorn doing the talking--Not your man-mate. And I've given it up--stopped two days ago in Tampico.

CHARMIAN: You are going to drink until it kills you.

JACK: No, this time it is for good. You have my word on it. I'm headed for a big adventure like the Klondike mate and I can't do it without you at my side.

CHARMIAN: To be used when you want and slapped aside when you don't. Suddenly I see it all very clearly.

[Charmian rips the last page out from between the rollers and hands it to him. She removes her glasses, fits the cover over her typewriter and starts packing away her things as he reads.]

Jack looks over the copy with growing concern.

JACK: I'd say we have hardly five hundred words if that?

VERACRUZ

CHARMIAN: If you want more than five hundred words, you had better write them. I think what I should do is book the first berth I can find back to Galveston.

JACK *[Shocked]:* Oh no, you can't do that!

CHARMIAN: Now I can, Jack, yes, not before but now I can. You betrayed us and all that is left are your appetites. They have devoured everything else, who you were, what we were together, what we stood for and our love Jack. Our love.

[Charmian stands up. Jack blocks her way. She tries to squeeze by him. He grabs her wrist.]

CHARMIAN: *[Hard]* Leave me be.

JACK: I love you, you know I do...

{Charmian steps around him, he grabs her, trying to embrace and kiss her.

Charmian punches him hard to his gut. Jack stumbles backwards from its force and the vehemence behind it. Charmian exits through the bedroom door, locking it behind her.}

BLACK OUT

ACT TWO; SCENE FOUR
THE PORTALES--EVENING

Jack enters and scans the tables. He spots Douglas, jodhpurs tailored in dashing British fashion, burnished leather holster on his hip sitting at a table with Captain Burnside. Jack joins them.

JACK: I just got your message, Doug.

   [Douglas rises and shakes Jack's hand.]

DOUGLAS: "Douglas," Jack, "Douglas." You know Captain Burnside?

   [Jack and Burnside shake hands. The waiter appears with Jack's bottle and glass; Jack waves him off.]

CAPTAIN BURNSIDE: Bravo on your latest dispatch, Mr. London. "May not a powerful enlightened nation stop a handful of incapable rulers from making a desert of their own fair land?" That one sentence of yours should be emblazoned on the front page of every newspaper in America. I left a copy on General Funston's desk.

DOUGLAS: I was just telling Captain Burnside of my adventure locating the engines. I dare say it is something you might appreciate.

JACK: I didn't mean to interrupt.

DOUGLAS: Always a pleasure to have the company of America's greatest writer. Now where was I Thomas? Yes, as I said, it was dark and squally when I left our lines, crossed the Boca del Rio in a native dugout and entered enemy territory. It took me a half-hour on foot to reach the rail line and, true to his word, the engineer was waiting at railhead with a handcart. He was also passed out drunk as a skunk. A couple of slaps got his mustache twitching and a couple more got him up and pumping with me on the handcart-- Well, down the line I found a pair of natives and hired them to do the pumping. I don't mind telling you those two kept eyeing my throat in the most suspicious manner. This wouldn't do, not if I was going to get to Alvarado and back by dawn, so I covered them with my automatic and searched them; relieving one of a vintage but very serviceable revolver, and the other of an equally efficient knife. Then I pulled out all my pockets so that they would know that even if they were able to slit my throat there would be nothing to reward them for it. So their only chance of remuneration was to get me back, safe and sound behind our lines. With this settled, the forty mile trip to Alvarado was strenuous if uneventful, although my Mexicans got increasingly nervous the deeper we went into enemy territory. At one point I had to put my Colt on them and tell them straight out that if they were scared about dying they better start pumping harder or they would.

CAPTAIN BURNSIDE: A dose of Dutch courage, right Jack?

JACK: Sounds like bare knuckled fear.

CAPTAIN BURNSIDE: Righto!

DOUGLAS: I found five engines hidden away on a siding right before Alvarado. Among them were two big, Baldwin pullers that passed my inspection with flying colors. No time to linger, I started back.

I hit trouble right upon leaving. Mexicans, the worst sort--no uniforms but armed with Mausers, bandoleers crisscrossing their chests, appeared out of nowhere. I made a break for it but they opened fire and pursued us. Three I left behind, but two stayed right on my tail, firing their Mausers. I had no choice but to put them down.

CAPTAIN BURNSIDE: Damn. Douglas, I wish I had been there.

ACT TWO; SCENE FOUR

DOUGLAS: I could have used some assistance because there was more to come.

Word must have gotten out because at Piedra, where the mist was so thick you couldn't see one end of the handcart from the other, I was surrounded by a dozen of them on horseback. One of my boys went down but I held the rest off bringing four down with my first clip. I don't mind telling you, I felt blessed when I found three bullet holes through my shirt but not even a scratch.

CAPTAIN BURNSIDE: Bully for you, Douglas!

DOUGLAS: Gents, it wasn't over yet. At Laguna, three more on horseback waylaid me from a siding. Two, I outdistanced easily but the third kept right along with me, managing to put another bullet through my shirt and two other slugs within six inches of my head.

BURNSIDE: You're lucky to have survived.

[Fred enters in the company of Walt Shepherd, a thin stoop-shouldered man in a seersucker suit that clings to him like a wet sheet. Fred spots Jack and, leaving Walt behind, heads over.]

DOUGLAS: Finally, I reached the Janampa river and started across. I was just breathing a sigh of relief when my boat hit a snag, capsized and sank. I'll tell you, I was so exhausted if I hadn't been in the shallows, I would have sunk too. It was all I could do to keep my wounded man's head afloat until I reached--

FRED: Jack, I've been looking for you.

JACK: Been up in Tampico lad, how you be.

FRED: I found out some things you might want to know about.

JACK *[To Doug and Burnside]:* Then out with it lad!

FRED: In private, Jack, I don't need any more interference from Captain MacArthur.

VERACRUZ

DOUGLAS *[Confident]:* You go ahead Jack, that's about all of it anyway.

JACK: If you will excuse me, gentleman.

[Jack rises and Fred ushers over to a table stage right.]

JACK: Compañero!

FRED: Jack, I have someone I want you to meet.

[Shepherd joins them.]

JACK: Jack London.

WALT: Walt Shepherd, Associated Press.

[They shake hands.]

FRED: Gents, have a seat.

[A waiter arrives.]

JACK: What's your poison?

WALT: A beer. Ah, hell, give me a shot too.

[Throughout Jack appears anxious to rejoin Douglas and Burnside.]

FRED: Tell him, Walt.

WALT: Big blond fellow in an ensign's uniform off the U.S.S. Arkansas, pals called him Boomer.

FRED: Bully.

WALT: Bully, Boomer, but I'll tell you Boomer fit him better--one of those guys never learned to talk, just shout.

You could hear him clear to N'Orleans!

FRED: That's him, right Jack? Him to a tee. Tell Jack what you heard, Walt, right here.

WALT: They were sitting over there-- all junior officers--about a dozen. Boomer was telling the others how he dealt with snipers they had caught. "I showed them the iron hand" is what he said.

JACK: What the hell. That could mean anything.

WALT: He was quite particular. Said he had his squad set their machine gun up at the end of the street and then they let the

ACT TWO; SCENE FOUR

Mexes out two at a time and gave them a chance to run for it. Counted to five before they opened up. Said a couple of the Mexes even thanked him for giving them a chance.

FRED: He say where?

WALT: Calle Rayón--right off the Malecón. Said they had 'em locked in a stable down there.

JACK: You didn't see him do it?

WALT: No, but I don't know why he'd be--

JACK *[To Fred]:* So what you're bringing me as proof is that Ensign Richardson, if it was the same ensign, told the same tale more than once which you have no evidence actually happened.

[Fred begins to lose it. People around them notice.]

FRED: Go down to Calle Rayón, look yourself. Damnit Jack! It's as plain as the nose on your face. Building walls pitted like you wouldn't believe.

JACK: Hell, my hotel room walls have bullet holes in them.

FRED: Not like these, Jack. Hardly any stucco left on them. Come on and I'll show you!

JACK: I have better ways to spend my time than wandering around Veracruz in the mid-day heat.

[Jack starts out of his chair.]

FRED: I don't get you, Jack. Bully confessed to it--no, he bragged about it and he told the same story on two different occasions. That's evidence enough. His word, as his type like to say, "As an officer and a gentleman"!

JACK: You heard the story in a whorehouse-- Walt heard it at a drinking party--I assume they weren't sipping tea when they told the story?

WALT: Only if it was out of rum bottles.

JACK: What about some of the other sailors involved? How about the Mexicans, the ones who made it to the corner? Get their testimony, then you have a story worth writing.

FRED: Now how the hell am I supposed to find them?

JACK: Fred, I thought you were a reporter. What about an interview with Bully --when he's sober?

FRED: Bully hasn't been let ashore and the rest of the sailors I tried to talk to gave me the brush-off. Your friend, Captain MacArthur, saw to that.

JACK: Admit it, Fred you don't have a story.

  [To Walt]

Did you write it up for the A.P.? I'll bet the ranch you didn't.

WALT: And get my ass fired--this ain't a great job but it's better than clerking in a shoe factory which was what I did before.

JACK: What you have, Fred, is a wish--a wish that you had a nice big story to write up-- but all you have are some drunken boasts of a loud-mouthed lad that you want to use for your own purposes. Fred, comrade to comrade: you know that I know that you know you don't have a story. Not one Jack London or any honest reporter would put their name to.

  [Jack starts to leave again but is stopped by Fred's words.]

FRED: I don't have a story you say, Jack London, well you're right there. I have two stories. First is the story that a U.S. Navy Ensign Bully Richardson, in his own words, on two separate occasions, confessed to the organizing of the shooting of Mexican prisoners of war in cold blood. The second story is about a revolutionary socialist who went to Mexico and was either hoodwinked or bribed by the oil boys or the bankers to make their brief for the conquest of this poor country.

  [Jack gets in his face. Formidable.]

JACK: Fred, here's the hard-fisted truth, you're nothing but a

ACT TWO; SCENE FOUR

sad victim of your own tangled reasoning in which neither Jack London nor the world has any interest.

FRED: Jack, how much did it take? Was it thirty pieces of silver or--

[Jack strikes out landing a right to Fred's chin, which sends him staggering backwards, knocking over table and chairs as he falls onto the stage, bleeding from the mouth. Jack stands over him, menacing.]

JACK: You sheeny bastard! Don't you dare talk to me that way. Why I've fought for--

[Fred throws Jack's words back at him.]

FRED: "I subscribe myself a chicken-thief and revolutionist." I can sure see the chicken-thief but what happened to the Revolutionist?

[Jack goes for him but Walt and a waiter grab him from behind. Jack shakes loose.]

JACK: You disgust me, you and your ghetto socialist comrades--Always ready to impart their twisted cant but nowhere when the fighting starts.

FRED: Why, Jack? Why!

WALT: Come on, Fred.

[Walt helps Fred to his feet. They exit.]

Jack straightens his clothes, lights a cigarette, and, ignoring the curious looks, rejoins Douglas and Captain Burnside.

JACK: My apologies, I suppose I made a spectacle of myself.

DOUGLAS: Not at all, Jack. Not at all. People know that type.

CAPTAIN BURNSIDE: I was saying that Douglas's adventure is worthy of a commendation.

DOUGLAS: Any American officer would have done--

CAPTAIN BURNSIDE: Douglas, You know the Navy's putting in their recommendations wholesale.

DOUGLAS: Yes I have heard. For The Congressional Medal of Honor no less.

CAPTAIN BURNSIDE: Ninety-two of them, all Navy and Marines. They sent Funston a copy of the list just to rub his nose in it.

DOUGLAS: I suppose my mission was as much under hostile conditions as the Navy landing.

CAPTAIN BURNSIDE: It certainly qualifies in that regard.

DOUGLAS: The problem is, I don't have any witnesses.

JACK: What about your Compañeros?

DOUGLAS: You mean my Mexicans? Who knows where they are now and besides, their testimony wouldn't count for much. No, I think it would be a waste of time.

CAPTAIN BURNSIDE: Well, it's a damn shame none of our own will--

DOUGLAS: I did tell Captain Cordier of my plans beforehand. Perhaps that might count for something.

CAPTAIN BURNSIDE: No reason he can't confirm the essentials of your mission. As intelligence officer, I'll write a letter as well. But first you have to file your report.

DOUGLAS: If I must, I must.

CAPTAIN BURNSIDE: The sooner the better. The President is demanding the list so he can announce the recipients. He wants some other picture on the front page of the newspapers besides those coffins coming home when he announces the withdrawal.

JACK *[Not sure he heard right]:* Withdrawal? What are you talking about?

DOUGLAS: President Wilson announced this morning that he has accepted the offer from Argentina, Chile and Brazil to arbitrate.

ACT TWO; SCENE FOUR

JACK: I'll be damned; You mean it's off.

DOUGLAS: I'm afraid so.

CAPTAIN BURNSIDE: Well, Douglas, I'm off to Bacci's to meet Miles and DeYoung. Will you join us?

DOUGLAS: I think not. I'm still a little worn out from my experience.

CAPTAIN BURNSIDE: That's wise to rest up, our constitution isn't meant for this climate. Mr. London, a pleasure to see you again. Douglas, I'll need your report by noon.

[Captain Burnside exits.]

JACK: I'll be goddamned, you said we were for sure going in.

DOUGLAS; Europe, Jack, that's where we're headed.

JACK: There won't be a white man left south of the Rio Grande.

DOUGLAS: I'm sure American interests will receive adequate guarantees.

JACK: The banks, the trusts, the oilmen, but the American pioneers, they'll be shipped back. Refugees in their own country. Back to a life of toiling to fill another man's pocket. To hell with them, to hell with their dreams!

DOUGLAS: Jack, this romantic notion of the American frontier getting a new start in Mexico--well, it's not practical, not in this new Century. America has to embrace nationalism, not lock horns with it. That was a lesson of our landing in Veracruz. It was the citizens of Veracruz, not the Mexican Army, who took up arms against us. Those transports that you see in the harbor whose cargo holds are filled with weaponry for our expeditionary forces? Their cargo will now serve as an inducement to responsible elements like Carranza, who are as much opposed to Villa and Zapata as we are, to protect our interests as well as their own.

JACK: So that's the plan, eh, create some tin-pot dictator of our own, load him up with guns and let him do our fighting for us.

VERACRUZ

DOUGLAS: Jack, you were bruising for a fight and so was I. But it is Europe now, Jack, where Caesar, Charlemagne, and Napoleon forged their destinies. There'll be some of your chesty action there for you to write about. You have my word on it.

[Douglas takes out an envelope.]

DOUGLAS: Jack, I have a favor to ask, could you give me your advice?

[He hands him his report]

I think it calls for more flair.

[Jack fits on his glasses and reads...]

JACK: "It was a dark and squally night when I left our lines, crossing the Boca del Rio in a native dugout." Why didn't you take the launch?

DOUGLAS: Excuse me?

JACK: The oil man, Buckley. Said he could get a launch to take you to Alvarado.

DOUGLAS: Oh, the bad weather. The launch captain didn't want to chance it. Jack, if I could prevail on you to give me some suggestions.

[Jack reads a little further.]

JACK: I've seen better tales in a boy's adventure magazine.

DOUGLAS: That's why I need your expertise. It's crucial that I achieve recognition for my participation in the Mexican campaign if I'm to get command of a regiment when hostilities break out in Europe. Important to you, too, as you will be at my side.

JACK: So that's the game?

DOUGLAS: With Wilson giving out medals by the dozen, it would surely count against me not to receive one.

JACK: I believed in you Doug; I believed there was a higher purpose.

ACT TWO; SCENE FOUR

DOUGLAS: God, Honor and Country, Jack, the words a soldier lives by.

[Douglas, adopting Bill Buckley's handshake, takes Jack's hand in both of his.]

DOUGLAS: Jack, not often a soldier can say at the end of a campaign that he has a new friend at his side. Shall we rendezvous later? It is probably not prudent for us to return to Sor Juana's but I'm sure you know of another.

[Douglas gives Jack's arm a squeeze and exits. Jack drops the report on the table.]

JACK: Compañero!

[The waiter appears with a bottle and glass for Jack.]

BLACK OUT

VERACRUZ

ACT TWO; SCENE FIVE
THE LONDON'S QUARTERS--LATER

Jack enters, disheveled, sweating rum. The room is empty, the bedroom door closed. Jack notes the newly made-up daybed and Charmian's luggage piled by the door. Jack tries the bedroom door. Locked. He BANGS on it with his fist.

JACK: It's over mate. Over. Wilson settled on arbitration. And to hell with the American Pioneers! To hell with them, eh?
   [Jack bangs some more. Charmian opens the door. She wears a bathrobe pulled tight.]
CHARMIAN: Is it the pioneers that upsets you or your own sorry dreams?
JACK: Mate, please.
CHARMIAN: And what about your heroic Captain did he desert you too?
JACK: I've been used. Treated like I was his houseboy or worse. Too hell with him. It's you I trust Mate.
CHARMIAN: I booked a berth to Galveston. It leaves at dawn.
JACK: I'll go too. We'll go back to Beauty Ranch where we belong. Just like you said devote myself to turning out good tales and get us out of debt.
CHARMIAN: I telegraphed the Sterlings. I'll be staying with them in San Francisco.
JACK: Charmian don't hold a grudge, not now.
   [She closes the door in Jack's face.]
JACK: Forgive me Mate. I try you know I try but I have his blood in me, the lesser race! I fight against it you know I have! Take your man-mate back! Take me back!
   [He bangs on it with both fists. Tears stream down Jack's

ACT TWO; SCENE FIVE

face. The force of his blows break the lock and the door flies open. Charmian faces him.]

CHARMIAN: Leave me be Jack.

JACK: I can't stop it when the bastard reigns, bastard me. Bastard Jack. A breed.

CHARMIAN: It's not your breeding. Not who your father was or was not. It's you Jack. You've betrayed your soul. What you were; what we were--together.

JACK: I wanted all of it, wanted it all.

CHARMIAN: And it's your wants have consumed you, or what you thought you wanted and now nothing's left.

JACK *[Pleading]:* We'll have a new beginning, The South Seas, mate, we'll take the Roamer to Tahiti, that's the place for us, for you and me. We'll renew ourselves, you have my pledge. It'll just be us, mate.

CHARMIAN: I loved you as a mate should. But you betrayed everything, your beliefs, me, but most of all yourself.

[Jack drops to his knees clinging to her robe. She resists being pulled toward him.]

JACK: I'll get my discipline back-- thousand words a day and we won't leave Beauty Ranch. Only if you say so.

CHARMIAN: I can't, Jack, I can't.

[She pushes him away.]

JACK: I'll do penance.

[He crosses the room on his knees, losing his balance, he falls face down. Righting himself, face bloodied, he continues.]

JACK: Penance, that's right, penance for pain I heaped on you.

[Reaching Charmian's writing table, he draws a pair of scissors out of their leather case and raises them to stab himself.]

VERACRUZ

[Charmian rushes toward him grabbing his arm. They struggle for the scissors.]

CHARMIAN: No Jack! No!

[Charmian gets the scissors away from him. He sinks defeated.{

JACK: Bastard Jack. Mongrel Jack.

CHARMIAN *[Softens]*: Jack it matters to no one else but you. What others know is the Jack London who made himself like no man ever has before and gives them hope they can. They know the Jack London who speaks for them. Whose words challenge presidents and kings. That is the Jack London in whom the world believes.

JACK: But I betrayed you mate. I betrayed you.

[Jack presses his head against her loins.]

CHARMIAN: Not you, not the true Jack London. No, the true Jack London would never betray his mate.

[The lights dim, the scrim falls, and we see them in silhouette. "We're off to Mexico" plays.]

BLACK OUT

ACT TWO; SCENE FIVE

EPILOGUE

The Actors Re-Assemble On Stage

CHARMIAN: Jack and Charmian resigned from the Socialist Party in the Spring of 1916: Jack died in the Fall at age 40. Charmian rejoined the Socialist Party two years later and spent the rest of her life protecting Jack's legacy. She died in 1952.

DOUGLAS: Douglas MacArthur died in 1964. Although he was America's most decorated general, MacArthur was not among the 55 servicemen who received the Medal of Honor in Veracruz.

FRED: Fred Boalt's article was published in the Memphis Press June 19, 1914.

BULLY: A court of inquiry held aboard the U.S.S. Texas exonerated Ensign William "Bully" Richardson and Fred Boalt was deported from Veracruz.

CHINA GIRL: When The U.S. Expeditionary Force evacuated Veracruz on November 23rd 1914 all the ladies went to see them off.

BILL: They left behind four warehouses stockpiled with 69,000 cubic yards of military equipment for Venustiano Carranza's Constitutionalist Forces who occupied the city.

SOR JUANA: Re-armed, the constitutionalists defeated the Zapata-Villa forces and seized effective control of Mexico.

BLACK OUT

END OF PLAY

SNOWBIRDS

SCENES

Act One

Scene One*:* *RV Park*
Scene Two: *RV Park - later*
Scene Three*:* *Interior RV - next morning*

Act Two

Scene One: *Interior RV*

CAST

Hal: *Retired Editor, 61*
Maggie: *College Professor, 52*
Dusty: *Snowbird, 60's*
Kelly-Ann: *Snowbird, 60's*
Inspector.: *Mexican Police, 28*

Voices over Caravan's C.B.
Wagonmaster: *Voice Only*
Other Snowbirds: *Voice Only*
Sergeante Martinez: *Voice Only*
Radio Operator: *Voice Only*
Capitan: *Voice Only*

SNOWBIRDS

ACT ONE; SCENE ONE
A MEXICAN RV PARK

Upstage is a rented motor home [RV] with the logo "GOIN' PLACES WITH SMILIN' FACES 1-800-RENT prominent on its side. It is either opaque or translucent depending on the location of the actors. Downstage is the 'lawn' in front of the RV where HAL LASS, shaggy hair going gray, a droopy mustache, and a thin frame presided over by a sedentary paunch, sits on a lime green and white webbed aluminum lawn chair, a cooler at his side, reading Picketty's "End of Capitalism': The First Five Thousand Years". He presses the stop function of the large, multi-function watch on his right wrist as

Stage Left: MAGGIE enters, back from a run. She is an attractive Hispanic woman, dark complexion and mid- fifties. She wears a faded "run-for-the-cure" tee shirt and running shorts. She stretches as they talk. Hal references the timer on his watch.

HAL: Twenty-eight minutes, thirty-three and three tenths of a second.

MAGGIE: It felt like forever.

HAL: The heat.

MAGGIE: I'm getting old.

HAL: We're in the right crowd.

MAGGIE: I thought it might be a kick to go to the meeting. They're having Karaoke after.

HAL: I don't think so.

MAGGIE: You have such a good voice.

HAL *[Sings with yiddish accent]*:

THE CLOAK MAKER'S UNION IS A NO-GOOD UNION,
A COMPANY UNION FOR THE BOSSES.
THEY PREACH SOCIALISM BUT PRACTICE FASCISM

ACT ONE; SCENE ONE

TO PRESERVE CAPITALISM -

MAGGIE: But your choice of material--

HAL: Gramp's favorite.

[Hal takes a fresh canned cocktail from the cooler.]

HAL: I made a survey on my walk. We're surrounded by patriots. Our RV is the only one without a flag plastered on it.

MAGGIE: I don't think it has the same implications as it used to.

HAL: Instead of kill the commies it's kill the rag heads?

MAGGIE: You're exaggerating.

HAL: Oh I don't think so but after years of living in our progressive little bubble I find it fascinating to be up close and personal with the "Homeland". For instance, the most popular bumper sticker is, " We're spending our children's inheritance"

MAGGIE: Black humor.

HAL: They hate their kids.

MAGGIE: There. You've already found you have something in common.

HAL *[laughs]:* I don't hate Frida. She thinks Ayn Rand rocks; I prefer Karl Marx.

MAGGIE: What's that you're drinking?

HAL: Cosmo. 1.99 a 4-PAC at Nogales Big Boys. Not bad.

[He offers Maggie the can. She takes a sip and spits it out.]

MAGGIE: If you like mouthwash.

[Stage left. DUSTY and KELLY-ANN, 60's, enter. They are a big, well-built couple with generous laughs. Dusty wears a tee shirt with 'I'm On Mexican Time' lettered on it in faded red and green and moves with a John Wayne swagger. Kelly-Ann wears Bermuda shorts, a gaily colored blouse and perhaps a straw, tourist sombrero. They both wear fanny-packs.]

DUSTY: How you folks doing this evening?

MAGGIE: Fine thanks.

DUSTY: I'm Dusty--my wife, Kelly-Ann. Ours is the next rig over.

MAGGIE: I'm Maggie.

HAL: Hal Lass.

[They shake hands.]

KELLY-ANN: First and Last, side by side whadya know. That's our last name, Fuerst, except you spell it F-u-e-r-s-t.

[Maggie laughs politely.]

DUSTY: Me and Kelly-Ann are your tail-gunners.

HAL: Are we likely to be strafed?

[Hearty laughter...]

DUSTY: Not likely. Must be your first trip?

HAL: First and last.

[This gets Guffaws.]

KELLY-ANN: You married a funny one, Maggie.

DUSTY: The tail-gunners bring up the rear. Somebody has mechanical trouble or illness or whatever, we drop out of line with them and see they get the help they need.

HAL: The designated good Samaritan.

DUSTY: Now that is exactly right.

KELLY-ANN: Well, mostly--we get fifty percent off our trip fees.

HAL: Well, then a fifty percent good Samaritan.

MAGGIE: Do you go to Mexico often?

DUSTY: Every winter.

KELLY-ANN: We just love it to death. The Mexican people are so great--`mi casa es su casa' and that's no lie. I hope you don't mind my asking but are you Mexican?

MAGGIE: I was born in Mexico. I grew up outside of Boston.

KELLY-ANN: That's America. We're from all over. Dusty's a Bohunk; I'm a Polack. How about you Hal where you from?

ACT ONE; SCENE ONE

HAL: The Pale.

DUSTY: Is that in Arizona?

HAL: Berkeley, California.

DUSTY: ...Well, we just wanted to drop by and say hi... Kelly-Ann, we ought to let these good people get about their business.

HAL: Hey, could I offer you a drink?

DUSTY: Why thank you but we better take a rain-check we got to get our butts over to the meeting-- Kelly-Ann's running for Sheriff.

HAL: Sheriffs, tail-gunners, who gets to be Pancho Villa?

KELLY-ANN: Why you Hal. You just let that mustache of yours grow a bit--Dusty will lend you one of his sombreros. Whadya think Maggie? Your hubby be a dead ringer for Pancho Villa.

MAGGIE: In his dreams.

DUSTY *[Patting Hal's paunch]*: Maybe Pauncho Villa.

KELLY-ANN: Dusty don't you get personal, we just met these folks.

HAL: No, I thank you. "Pauncho Villa". I've been trying to think of a handle for our C.B. I was thinking of Jew--

MAGGIE *[Interrupts]*: You were saying about the sheriff?

KELLY-ANN: It's just caravan thing, honey. The Sheriff makes sure everyone is doing O.K. You know, keep everything moving. When somebody's late to a tour or doesn't come to a get-together, or just whatever, the sheriff fines them a few pesos and at the end of the trip we either have a party or give it to a worthy charity.

DUSTY: Kelly-Ann..?

KELLY-ANN: We'll see you later. If you have any questions, problems, you just come knocking, hear?

[Dusty takes Kelly-Ann by the hand.]

DUSTY: Ditto that.

[They exit stage right. As Maggie slips on a pair of warm-up pants.]

HAL: The Bohunk and the Polack snuggled right up next to what? The kike and the wetback? Now isn't that America?

MAGGIE: I wish you wouldn't use ethnic slurs.

HAL: Maggie, don't you get tired of being so politically correct?

MAGGIE: I'm tired of racism.

HAL: No worries. Haven't you heard? We're a post-racial society.

MAGGIE: You sure you don't want to come? It'll be fun. Get to know your fellow travelers.

HAL: Do you really want to get to know Dusty and Kelly-Ann?

MAGGIE: Why not?

HAL: Because they are ignorant mid-western Babbits, who use ethnic slurs.

MAGGIE: Later.

HAL *[Toasting her with his Cosmo]:* You have my proxy vote-- The Polack for sheriff!

[Maggie flips him off as she exits. Hal drains his cosmo, hoists himself off the chair, grabs his towel and the toilet kit that is hanging from the rope awning and exits.]

BLACK OUT

ACT ONE; SCENE TWO
CAMP SITE-LATER

Hal, changed and showered, exits the RV, a bag of chips in one hand a can of DEET in the other. He settles back in his chair, sprays around him and pops another Cosmo. Maggie enters.

HAL: How was it?

MAGGIE: Fun.

HAL: Did you toast marshmallows?

MAGGIE: No.

HAL: Sing Kumbaya?

MAGGIE: The Internationale.

HAL: And how did our Polack do?

MAGGIE: Kelly-Ann ran unopposed and fined you twenty pesos for missing the karaoke. They're some interesting people in the group. One couple--a little older than us. She's a painter and-

HAL: Landscapes or cats?

MAGGIE: Hal, why did you want to do this in the first place?

HAL: Bring Luciano his ecological shitter.

MAGGIE: We could have shipped it. I would have been more than happy to fly.

HAL: Lighten up, I'm joking. We always fly. I'm really, enjoying our road trip... Traveling through the heartland with my beloved, sampling the subtle cuisines of the 'all-you-can-eat' buffets, and now a fish in the sea of timeless Mexico where mi casa es su casa.

[Hal leads Maggie in a waltz. Across the stage. They move effortlessly together.]

HAL *[Loud]:*

ARISE YE PRISONERS OF STARVATION

ARISE YE WRETCHED OF THE EARTH!

MAGGIE *[But amused]:* Hal, shhh, it's late.

HAL *[Softly, close dancing]:*

SOMEONE'S SLEEPING, MY LORD, KUMBAYA
OH LORD, KUM--.

[Hal stumbles but manages a controlled fall back into his chair, without spilling his Cosmo.]

MAGGIE: Jeez Hal, how many of those have you had?

HAL: They sort of creep up on you.

MAGGIE: Oh, guess what? We're going to be stuck in a roadblock most of tomorrow.

HAL: Say what?

MAGGIE: The Federales have set up a roadblock. They say it's drug related.

HAL: Are they searching tourists?

MAGGIE: I guess.

HAL: Shit.

MAGGIE: Así es la vida.

HAL: What?

MAGGIE: That's life.

HAL: I don't think it was smart bringing all this stuff down for Luciano.

MAGGIE: They're looking for drugs not toilets.

HAL: We should have paid the duty.

MAGGIE: Oh come on--what happened to my fire breathing revolutionary?

[Massaging his shoulders.]

MAGGIE: Chinga Los Pinche Federales!

HAL: I've had enough of this caravan business --lets cut out on our own. I wouldn't mind spending a couple of days in San Luis Potosi.

ACT ONE; SCENE TWO

MAGGIE: We still have to go through the roadblock. It's set up in both directions.

HAL: That's a problem.

MAGGIE: People bring things for their families all the time. Everyone tries to avoid paying duties. At worst we'll pay a fine.

[Maggie nuzzles Hal, kissing his neck.]

MAGGIE: What do you say to a little connubial bliss?

[Hal doesn't respond. Maggie feels rebuffed.]

HAL: Maggie, I told you I've been working with this new solidarity group?

MAGGIE: The one about political prisoners?

HAL: No, they turned out to be a bunch of letter writing liberals. This is a group that formed in solidarity with Nahuatl communities in the Sierra who are opposing the construction of a toll road through their communal lands.

MAGGIE: Sort of... You had an event last month on campus with that singer?

HAL: Michael Frante. He didn't show--neither did you.

MAGGIE: Right, I had some sort of conflict.

HAL: You didn't want to be bothered.

MAGGIE: We gave some money-- didn't we?

HAL: Yes---Did you read that article I e-mailed about the massacre at Cuatepec.

MAGGIE: No. I must have missed it. What happened?

HAL: A group of villagers on their way to the municipio to file claims against the land seizures were ambushed by PRI thugs. Ten were killed, three of them children.

MAGGIE: How horrible.

HAL: It galvanized the resistance. Self defense units have been formed. Villagers are blocking construction sites sabotaging equipment and anything they can think of to stop the construction of the road. Basically, it's low intensity warfare.

MAGGIE: Hopefully they'll work out a compromise.

HAL: Nobody's in the mood to compromise.

MAGGIE: Then the government will crush them.

HAL: Not if they can arm themselves.

MAGGIE: Resulting in the usual death and mayhem--like Oaxaca and they weren't even armed.

HAL: In Chiapas the Zapatistas were armed and now are a political force to be reckoned with.

MAGGIE: What transformed the EZLN into a national political force was Marcos' use of the media. The guns were essentially props.

HAL: Campesinos in ski-masks with AK-47s chasing the army out of San Cristobal de las Casas sounds like an armed insurrection to me.

MAGGIE: It was an act of theater.

HAL: I didn't know they used live ammunition in theater.

MAGGIE: Viva Los campesinos. I'm going to bed.

[A kiss on the forehead]

Remember to lock up.

HAL: Some of the members of our solidarity group go back and forth between the U.S. and the Sierras.

MAGGIE: It must be dangerous.

HAL: They're gutsy.

MAGGIE: 'Night

As she heads for the RV.

HAL: Maggie, after I rented the RV, I left it with them over the weekend.

MAGGIE: What for?

ACT ONE; SCENE TWO

HAL: I didn't see any reason to tell you.

MAGGIE: Tell me what?

HAL: Well I, uh, volunteered.

MAGGIE: Hal what's going on? Do you have a bunch of propaganda stashed in our RV. We should have discussed this.

HAL: Actually, in your terms if Zapatistas' weapons were an act of theater you could call it propaganda of a sort. There's no risk really--we're the perfect couple--except now this roadblock.

MAGGIE: What is in our RV, Hal? If we get caught with a bunch of incendiary propaganda we could get in a real mess.

HAL: It's not propaganda.

MAGGIE: Then what is it? Oh Christ you didn't--that's crazy-no impossible... Hal!

HAL: I did exactly what I have been saying needs to be done.

MAGGIE: Hal what is in our RV!

HAL: Guns, semiautomatics mostly, we've been buying at gun shows around--

MAGGIE: My God! Oh, my God!

HAL: You weren't supposed to know. When we stopped in Guadalajara I'd tell you I was taking the RV to have the brakes checked or something. They'd unload them and that would be that. Except now I got scared and blurted it out--

MAGGIE: I don't understand how you could do this.

HAL: You haven't been listening.

MAGGIE: It's hard not to: Revolution! Revolution! Occupy! Since you retired you've been sounding like some demented street corner preacher with stains on his pants.

HAL: Like the ones in Sproul Plaza. If you listened to them, their politics have a populist---

MAGGIE: You son of a bitch!

[Maggie loses it, striking him with her fists. A few hard blows to face and chest, before he grabs her wrists. Maggie pushes him away.]

HAL: You can take a cab back to Zacatecas. I'll run the roadblock alone.

MAGGIE: The first thing they'll ask is where I am.

HAL: You got sick. Went home. We had a fight--that's even the truth.

MAGGIE: You don't even speak Spanish!

HAL: Enough to say that... If you look at it logically there is really nothing to worry about.

MAGGIE: An RV full of weapons and nothing to worry about! Who are these people, your new found compañeros

HAL: Everyone goes by a nomme de guerre.

MAGGIE: Tell me! I'm their damn mule!

HAL: The group doesn't have a name. Part of their anti-hierarchical--

MAGGIE: I can guess. I pass them everyday hanging out at the cafes. International lumpen bourgeoisie of the world arise! You have nothing to lose but your allowances!...
Perfect. Pauncho Villa and the pretenders!

HAL: They remind me of us--when we both believed in revolution.

MAGGIE: We didn't run guns.

HAL: We considered it.

MAGGIE: We considered a lot of things.

HAL: We supported armed struggle.

MAGGIE: And where did it get anybody?

HAL: Listen Maggie, I'm sorry I involved--

MAGGIE: Which one's the police informer?

HAL: It's a tight group. They're very security conscious.

ACT ONE; SCENE TWO

MAGGIE: Then why the hell are they dealing with you?

HAL: I'm one of them.

MAGGIE: Hal, for the last quarter century we have been living in a brown shingled bungalow on a tree-lined street in a pretty college town where you went every day to work editing the university alumni magazine. I don't see revolution. I see a politically responsible middle-class life. Maybe I'm missing something. Perhaps you were underground?

HAL: I was in denial.

MAGGIE: And now you've emerged from your barco-lounger as Commandante Hal of the revolutionary mid-life crisis brigade!

HAL: I think of it as my Paul, Chevroleting to Damascus moment.

MAGGIE: You're deranged.

HAL: Society's label of convenience for its revolutionaries.

MAGGIE: Who do you think you are? Lenin? Trotsky?

HAL: Nothing so stinging as the contempt of the formerly radical.

MAGGIE: How could I be so stupid, you're Ché.

HAL: "Let me say, with the risk of appearing ridiculous, that a true revolutionary is guided by strong feelings of love." Remember? You wrote it out and pasted it on the wall over our bed in Cambridge.

MAGGIE: That was thirty years ago.

HAL: That makes it no longer true? Maggie join me, no, rejoin me in the struggle.

[Hal reaches for her; she shrinks back.]

MAGGIE: I feel like I've been mugged by a time warp.

HAL: By reality. This isn't some abstraction, these are mothers, fathers, children, fighting to maintain their land, their dignity, their culture. I could no more turn my back on them any more than we could on the Vietnamese.

MAGGIE: I can see the headlines, "University Couple Caught Running Guns."

HAL: We won't get caught.

MAGGIE: Hal, you must have had some kind of break.

HAL: Bullshit.

MAGGIE: That's the only sense I can make of it.

HAL: One too many free trade lattes drove me over the edge.

MAGGIE: Not funny.

HAL: Or maybe it was staring at too many pithy bumper stickers: "Speak truth to Power?" How can anybody possibly think telling our government the truth would produce anything more than a smirk?

MAGGIE: It's a metaphor for standing up.

HAL: With a bumper sticker? Little did I know that in moving to Berkeley I was entering the radicals' Never-Never-Land.

MAGGIE: We moved so I could take the job at the University.

HAL: I'm not blaming you. I allowed myself to be lulled into complacency.

MAGGIE: Why didn't you do something about it? You could have quit the magazine. I don't know how many times I urged you to take a leave of absence and write something you valued.

HAL: Working for the magazine wasn't the problem. It was the totality of my life. Without ever making a decision, there I was on the sidelines, immobilized by the ether of political correctness that wafts over our righteous community of do-goodness where there's always a pleasant demo or a picket line to join or a peaceful sit-in to get arrested at. I took pleasure in separating my recyclables, buying green and reading those clever bumper stickers. "Mommy, what's a tree?" Was a favorite. Then Occupied happened and like Rip Van Winkle, I woke up.

ACT ONE; SCENE TWO

MAGGIE: O.K. so that's you. By what right do you make me your accomplice?

HAL: None. I got caught up in the moment and --uh--I agreed to do it.

MAGGIE: You mean you agreed we'd do it.

HAL: The original plan was for Jai--a young couple in our group to make the run --One of them had been arrested last year in Oaxaca but they were still willing to do it despite the personal danger. I was sitting there as they were making plans for the trip and, well, I thought if there was ever a time for me to step in and make a commitment to what I believed--this was it. So I volunteered. There wasn't any pressure. Everyone was grateful that I had fronted for them at the gun shows--

MAGGIE: You bought the guns?

HAL: It made sense. Who would suspect an old white dude with a flag on his lapel?

MAGGIE: Actually, it makes no sense at all.

HAL: They'd most likely get caught; I wouldn't.

MAGGIE: What did your collective think about involving me?

HAL: We put it to a vote. It wasn't unanimous--I had qualms about not telling you-- so did a couple of the others-- but in military matters we're democratic centralist so ultimately it was my decision as well.

MAGGIE: Great, I'm married to some Stalinist who has no problem using his wife as a Judas goat.

HAL: You're exaggerating.

MAGGIE: Yes I suppose it could be worse--you could have become a serial killer.

HAL: Come on.

MAGGIE: I just can't believe this!

HAL: I tried to talk about what I was feeling- my analysis- but you didn't want to hear any of it. The second time around Obama was going to fix everything was the perceived truth and any opinions to the contrary were about as welcome as a fart at a hot tub party. You think I was unaware of those sympathetic glances between you and your friends when I dared question it? Not even doing me the courtesy of disagreeing.

MAGGIE: So as to be insulted by you. Hal you don't discuss, you harangue.

HAL: I think when you got tenure you felt it vested you with ultimate wisdom.

MAGGIE: You resented it.

HAL: I gave you a dozen red roses.

MAGGIE: With a card congratulating me for achieving "ultimate institutional installation."

HAL: I was being funny.

MAGGIE: Snarky.

HAL: I love you Maggie and admire you for who you are and what you accomplished. I suppose I was hoping that in your heart you would support-

MAGGIE: Support bringing guns for people to kill each other. How could you expect me to support that knowing how my parents died?

HAL: Your parents are alive and well in Boston.

MAGGIE: My birth parents.

HAL: If they had weapons, they could have defended themselves.

MAGGIE: According to Luciano, they did, so instead of just being thrown off their land they were murdered as well.

HAL: You no longer believe people have a right to resist; a right to armed self-defense?

MAGGIE: I don't question their right but I know the results and

ACT ONE; SCENE TWO

have the nightmares to remind me. I don't want any part of this. None.

HAL: I told you if there's any problem I'll take full responsibility--

MAGGIE: What right do you have to inject yourself into a situation in which you have no risk.

HAL: The community requested the guns and as for risk I'm sitting on it.

MAGGIE: You mean we're sitting on it.

HAL: I believe we have a revolutionary-

MAGGIE: The revolution was a failure. Berlin Wall. Prague Spring. The Gang of Four. Two million dead Cambodians! Whatever the answer is to the horror our government and others are perpetuating on the world, armed revolution is not it!

HAL: The Chinese people are certainly a lot better off after their revolution. Vietnam? Cuba? For all their faults they are more just societies after their revolutions than before. And Venezuela where--

MAGGIE: They shut down the free press?

HAL: The CIA subsidized press.

MAGGIE: Just because some leader spouts a bunch of anti-Yankee rhetoric doesn't make him a revolutionary. More often than not it makes him a demagogue.

HAL: It's not inevitable.

MAGGIE: Then why is it the way it usually turns out.

HAL: You don't fight oppression and injustice because you're going to win; you fight it because it's wrong!

MAGGIE: But you don't have to run crates of guns to Mexico without telling your wife especially when they are in the RV with you!

HAL: Maggie, all I can do is ask your forgiveness.

MAGGIE: Fuck-off.

[Brushing past him; Maggie exits into the RV, leaving a stunned, gob-smacked Hal in her wake. Hal stumbles about cleaning up but mostly keeping an eye on the RV.]

[Light Change. Interior RV]

[Maggie sits up on the futon in her bathrobe rubbing skin cream on her face. Hal enters with the cooler. He sets it down and locks the RV door as Maggie arranges herself for a night in the passenger seat.]

HAL: You must admit the risk is minimal?... Mags, I'm sorry I got you into this. I should have kept my mouth shut about the guns... Listen, really you could take a bus...The silent treatment. O.K.

[Hal undresses, gets under the covers and turns his back. Lights down.]

MAGGIE: It wasn't enough you destroyed your own life, you wanted to make sure you destroyed mine as well.

HAL: Nobody's life is destroyed--you weren't supposed to know.

MAGGIE: I understand at 18 why I wanted to screw you but how could I have been dumb enough to marry you?

HAL: Sometimes one-night stands last a lifetime.

MAGGIE: Not this one.

BLACK OUT

ACT ONE; SCENE THREE

ACT ONE; SCENE THREE
INTERIOR RV - NEXT MORNING

Hal snores on the futon; Maggie sits behind the wheel, fuming.

WAGONMASTER [O.S.]: Good morning snowbirds; We're ready to roll! Vehicle one.

[Maggie starts the ENGINE. Hal rolls over and sits up, head in hands as the roll call continues.]

BORN FREE [O.S.]: Born Free presente.

WAGONMASTER [O.S.]: Vehicle two?

SUGAR SHACK [O.S.]: Sugar Shack presente.

[Hal heaves himself up off the bed, and careens into the W.C. His undershirt almost covers his bare ass.]

HAL: Oh my head...

[Maggie listens to him 'ride the train' with grim satisfaction.]

WAGONMASTER [O.S.]: Vehicle three.

OUR CASTLE [O.S.]: Our Castle presente.

WAGONMASTER [O.S.]: Vehicle four.

MY WAY [O.S.]: My Way presente.

WAGONMASTER [O.S.]: Vehicle five.

MAGGIE: Pauncho Villa here.

WAGONMASTER *[Total Anglo accent]:* No hablo inglés. Pauncho Villa/

MAGGIE: *[Exaggerated accent]:* Pauncho Villa presente.

WAGONMASTER [O.S.]: Vehicle six.

DUSTY: Tail-Gunner presente.

WAGONMASTER [O.S.]: Snowbirds, lock and load! We're good to go.

[Maggie shifts into gear and follows the others into traffic. Hal exits the W.C.]

MAGGIE: You were putting me on last night?

HAL: Right.

[Hal chases a mega-dose of aspirin with a bottle of water.]

MAGGIE: You're lying.

HAL: I'm sorry Maggie, I got scared and blurted it out.

MAGGIE: Anything else you want to unburden yourself with-- like you're wearing a suicide vest? I can't believe you'd do this.

HAL: Don't think about it. We're a pair of geezers with a bunch of other geezers taking their RVs to Mexico for a winter vacation. We're fucking snowbirds. Mr. and Mrs. Normal.

MAGGIE: You've put my whole life in jeopardy.

HAL: If anything happens, I'll take full responsibility.

MAGGIE: Hal, I'm in the RV, my name is on the lease, and I will be arrested. And when the University, who hate my guts anyway, finds out, they'll fire--

HAL: LOOK OUT!

[HORNS. Maggie brakes, swerves--HORNS ETC- an almost accident.]

MAGGIE: You always were arrogant but this I can't understand. How you could involve me in this. It's like some absurdist farce.

HAL: If I had a dollar for every time a revolutionary movement has been called absurd or a farce, I'd be richer than the proverbial capitalist pig.

MAGGIE: My, my, all the old rhetoric coming back.

HAL: It suits me better.

MAGGIE: When you were twenty and brash; not sixty and senile!

ACT ONE; SCENE THREE

HAL *[Acting it]:* Has mommy made coffee?

MAGGIE: Choke on it. And put on some pants!

[Hal slips on a pair of baggy shorts.]

MAGGIE: Where are these, these guns?

HAL: Well hidden.

MAGGIE: We'll have to find a way to ditch them.

HAL: Maggie we'll be fine. This is completely beneath the radar. Think about it. The CIA, FBI. Whoever, are too busy waterboarding Arabs to bother with us--at least for now.

MAGGIE: What if they search us?

HAL: They won't as long as we don't give them any cause-- They might look around a bit but they certainly aren't going to pull the RV apart.

MAGGIE: Unless they know what they are looking for. Have you thought about what it would be like to spend the rest of your sorry life in a Mexican jail. Both of us!

HAL: If we were infiltrated they would have busted us already... How many cars ahead of us?

MAGGIE: Look.

[Hal opens a window or door and looks out.]

HAL: A lot. By the time they get to us they'll be too tired to search.

MAGGIE: What if I tell them?

HAL: You wouldn't, Maggie.

MAGGIE" "May I introduce you to the great revolutionary leader Commandante Pauncho, who, on the outside chance you don't know already, has a case of guns under the floor.

HAL: You couldn't live with yourself.

MAGGIE: Is that where they are, under the floor? Tell me! I want them out of here!

HAL: I can't do that.

MAGGIE: You don't know where they are.

HAL: I didn't want to know--

MAGGIE: Asshole!

WAGONMASTER [O.S.]: Listen up snowbirds, our Sheriff had a pow-wow with the roadblock commandante and she's worked out an arrangement with him to bring us through as a group. We've been instructed to pull our rigs off just up ahead at the 560 klik marker and wait for the commandante's men to check our papers and escort us through. Now do I hear a big thanks and a God bless for Sheriff Kelly-Ann and her side-kick Dusty!

HAL: Pauncho Villa here! Three cheers for Kelly-Ann and Dusty!

ALL [O.S.]: Roger that! You got that right!

HAL: Commandante Pauncho to Dusty and Kelly-Ann... Uh, ten-four.

DUSTY [O.S.]: I read you Pauncho-Ten-four.

HAL: Two long cool ones are waiting for you at Casa Pauncho!

DUSTY [O.S.]: I can already taste them.

[Maggie steers the RV off the road, stops and turns off the engine. She puts her head down on the steering wheel letting the tension drain out.]

HAL: See, Mags, we're cool--way cool.

[Hal offers her a water from the fridge. She ignores it.]

MAGGIE: How did this happen Hal? I need to understand.

HAL: Do you ever think about our wedding?

MAGGIE: Lately, with deep regret.

HAL: Fists raised, singing the ANC Anthem loud enough for Nelson Mandela and the comrades imprisoned on Robbin Island to hear! "To the Revolution!" Friends shouted and we replied, "Whatever it takes!" Whatever it takes!

MAGGIE: And I've carried those ideas into my work.

ACT ONE; SCENE THREE

HAL: We sold out.

MAGGIE: We grew up, at least I did. I never stopped being politically active. Despite your sneers I've worked for every progressive Democratic candidate that-

HAL: Progressive Democrat is a contradiction in terms.

MAGGIE: How about guns and peace?

HAL: Mags, I was wrong to involve you--no matter how little the risk. I wish to hell I hadn't. I just didn't...

MAGGIE: It's between us now and I don't see how we'll ever overcome it. I don't.

HAL: Come on Mags, I made a mistake, O.K? Minimized the risk. It's my arrogance. We know I have that tendency... Not in my furthest imagination did I believe there would be trouble--and now we know there won't be.

[Hal takes her hand. After a beat she pulls away.]

MAGGIE: Hal I always trusted you. No matter how crazy it got between us you'd look out for me and I for you. What are we after thirty years, strangers? Because that's what it feels like.

HAL: ...Remember when Carlos and Roberto organized a group to fight on the southern front?

MAGGIE: I remember when Roberto resurfaced as a leading Sandinista. And I remember Carlos' little boy crying his heart out at the memorial for his father.

HAL: They wanted me to go with them.

MAGGIE: You never told me.

HAL: We joined a shooting range, worked out, went on forced marches, practiced hand-to-hand combat.

MAGGIE: You were really going to go with them?

HAL: That was my plan.

MAGGIE: And what? Frida and I would wake up one morning and there'd be a note on the pillow?

HAL: I was planning to tell you--I kept putting it off because I didn't want to face it--I knew how upsetting...but anyway when it came down to it I was too chicken-shit to go anyway--I backed out.

MAGGIE: You couldn't have gone. Frida had just been born.

HAL: Yes, that's what I told myself. I was scared.

MAGGIE: Who wouldn't be.

HAL: Others overcame it.

MAGGIE: Hal, you had a family.

HAL: So did Carlos as you remembered. What I am trying to tell you, Maggie, is at the moment when the essence of everything I had been saying and believed in boiled down to taking action, I failed. I didn't tell you then because I was ashamed of myself and now, thirty years later a young couple with their whole lives ahead of them are willing to risk everything for the sake of others and all I could think was: Why not me. This time around, no more excuses. Telling you would just be a way of backing out again.

[KNOCKS on the door make them both jump.]

DUSTY [O.S.] Hola Pauncho.

[Light change; exterior]

[Hal exits the RV. And greets Dusty and Kelly-Ann with exaggerated bonhomie.]

HAL: Why goodness, it's the neighbors, Mags, come over for a visit!

DUSTY: Visit, heck we're looking for those cold big ones you were talking about.

HAL: Coming right up. Ahorita. We'll have a victory celebration uber Federales. Wait just a gosh-darn second and I'll grab the cooler.

[Hal exits into the RV as Maggie enters.]

ACT ONE; SCENE THREE

DUSTY; Hi there, Maggie.

KELLY-ANN: Thank you kindly for inviting us over. After a few days on the road, between two of you, there's not much left to be said worth listening to. Poor Dusty, I've been talking up a storm.

MAGGIE: Thanks so much for speeding us through the roadblock.

KELLY-ANN: No problem, that Captain Ramirez is a good old boy. He doesn't want to waste his time with us.

MAGGIE: How long do you think before we get going?

Hal returns lugging the cooler with folding chairs balanced on top. He sets them down, then unfolds the chairs as the conversation continues.

KELLY-ANN: Captain Ramirez promised by one o'clock, so we can make it to the RV park before dark.

DUSTY: Mexican time that's four.

KELLY-ANN: Dusty.

DUSTY: No offence.

HAL: Bar's open.

[Hal flips up the cooler lid, inviting Dusty to help himself.]

DUSTY: There you go!

[Dusty pulls out a Tecate.]

HAL: Don't be shy Kelly-Ann. What could I get you?

KELLY-ANN: Thank you kindly. I'll take one of those waters.

MAGGIE: I'll have one too.

[Hal obliges and pulls a water for himself.]

HAL: A toast to our sheriff and her good works!

DUSTY: And new friends!

[Hal makes a point of touching cans/bottles with the others.]

DUSTY: How are you folks enjoying the open road?

KELLY-ANN: Not that today is very open.

HAL: Speaking for myself, Kelly-Ann, I just love it to death--especially with my better half doing the driving.

[Toasting again]

To the open road & new adventures!

KELLY-ANN: Me and Dusty were talking and couldn't help but wonder whether you folks in the movie business?

MAGGIE: No, we're from Northern California.

KELLY-ANN: Hal sure does look like one of those producer types, you know, that you see during the Academy Awards and Dusty was saying that you're a dead-ringer for the gal who was in West Side Story. You know the one I mean--

HAL: Rita Moreno?

KELLY-ANN *[She winks at Hal]*: Dusty had a crush on her so you better watch out.

HAL: And you Dusty, right around the eyes especially, look just like the Duke.

KELLY-ANN: Everyone tells him that.

DUSTY *[A passable imitation]*: Pilgrim, what do you do back across the Rio Grande?

HAL: I worked for a university alumni magazine.

DUSTY: Writing seems a nice way to make a living, if you have the talent for it.

HAL: Writing has nothing to do with what I did. My days were spent churning out obsequious drivel about the "accomplishments" of illustrious, meaning rich alumni and shilling at the President's receptions where I was required to listen to boozy old boy memories. If I had to do it all over I'd shoot myself.

DUSTY: A couple boys I coached went on to play for your university. Jack Schmidt, he was a tight end, and Mike Saunders--point guard--almost made All-American.

ACT ONE; SCENE THREE

HAL: Did they become rich?

DUSTY: Not those two -- dumb as doorstops.

HAL: Then I didn't write about them.

DUSTY: You must have been one happy camper when your retirement came round.

HAL: I didn't actually retire. My leaving was an inadvertent result of the chancellor's annual homecoming party that he hosted with Trevor "Cubbie" Townsend IV, former star quarterback and "Major Donor". Cubby guzzled too much of the chancellor's single malt, then plowed his Chinese red '58 Jag into a goiter ridden chestnut tree planted by the class of '83--that's 1883.

The Chancellor, a gimlet eye trained on a final bequest from the widow, ordered the university flags flown at half mast and "suggested" that the staff wear black mourning bands on their sleeves. My contribution was a poem commemorating the occasion:

"Cubbie jumped in his Jag, not a care in the world.

When he plowed into that crusty old bough.

Cubbie's pate met trunk with a terrible thunk

Showering pieces all over the ground.

Strange, many exclaimed, bone and bark everywhere

But a brain nowhere was found."

Unfortunately, an assistant editor, who wanted my job, posted it anonymously on the alumni web page but everyone knew who wrote it. The chancellor fired me but "On the advice of counsel" that was changed to early retirement. Since then I've--

MAGGIE: And you folks, are you still working?

KELLY-ANN: Retired, mostly. Dusty coached high school football and taught metal shop. I was a cop.

MAGGIE & HAL: Really?

KELLY-ANN: I've pension to show for it. Twenty-two years in the juvenile division of Iowa City police department.

MAGGIE: That must have been interesting.

KELLY-ANN: Sad mostly, some you could help but most, their lives were already ruined. I can cry just thinking about some of them. Dusty and me --we never had kids so, you know, I got real attached to some.

DUSTY: You folks have children?

HAL: Not any longer.

KELLY-ANN: Oh, I'm sorry.

HAL: Not dead--out of the house. The experience is over-rated.

DUSTY: I never heard anybody say that before.

MAGGIE: And I don't agree.

DUSTY: Aw Hal's just kidding.

MAGGIE: No he's not. Last time he saw out daughter he threw a glass of wine in her face.

HAL: We had a political argument. I was explaining that the key purpose of staying in Afghanistan was to provide security for a Sunoco oil pipeline from the Caspian Sea to the Persian Gulf thereby cutting the Russo/ Chinese cartels out of the loop and our daughter gets on her cell and buys a thousand shares of Sunoco. Then she tells me I'm a senile wind-bag.

MAGGIE: After you called her a bloodsucking war profi-teer...

HAL: We'll patch it up. I'll call her on her birthday.

MAGGIE: You said that last year...

[An embarrassed silence. Hal drains his water and pulls himself out a cosmo.]

DUSTY: ..Kelly-Ann what were their names? The couple from Abilene in the Air-Stream who drank those? Canned heat. That's what they called them.

ACT ONE; SCENE THREE

KELLY-ANN: The Whitmans.

DUSTY: Whitmans, right. Last time we saw them they were drinking Sprite. Said their doctors told them they needed new livers.

KELLY-ANN: Don't let Dusty scare you. They were drinking morning to night. It's a wonder they were able to keep their rig on the road.

MAGGIE: I'm the designated driver.

KELLY-ANN: You go girl! I tell him one brewski, I'll go with that. Two, I'm behind the wheel.

DUSTY: Maggie, you still on the 40 hour drill team?

MAGGIE: I teach at the University.

HAL: Global theory.

DUSTY: You don't say.

KELLY-ANN: That's real interesting, especially way things are, you know.

HAL: Kelly-Ann, I don't know.

KELLY-ANN: Well, Iraq and all. The Axis of Evil. Iran. Goodness gracious, Hal, you all must be scared to death what they want to do to your people, you know--just like Hitler.

HAL: You think I'm Jewish?

KELLY-ANN: No offence, I just love the Jewish people to death. Our church, you know, gives regularly so that Jewish people from Russia can return to their homeland.

DUSTY: Kelly-Ann's a profiler. She can tell you things you don't even know about yourself.

[Maggie & Hal: alarm bells.]

MAGGIE: I thought you were retired?

KELLY-ANN: I lasted six months. Baked so many brownies I was bursting my jeans,

DUSTY: Mine too.

KELLY-ANN: I had to do something, you know, and Homeland Security was opening an office in Iowa City so I applied. I told them January through March I'm gone. They were real nice about it. Sent me to language school to learn Arabic and trained me to do profiles.

HAL: And who do you profile? Unless that's confidential.

KELLY-ANN: You know, you get a name and then you run it through the different data bases and other sources related to terrorist activity and come up with a score.

MAGGIE: Score for what?

KELLY-ANN: Terrorist potential. You know, the likelihood of it on a scale of one to ten.

HAL: What do you consider?

KELLY-ANN: That's confidential, Hal, but pretty much things you'd expect.

DUSTY: And plenty you wouldn't--That's for darn sure.

HAL: Well, what would you give us on a one-to ten?

KELLY-ANN: You and Maggie, you mean if they sent me your names?

HAL: Right.

KELLY-ANN: Probably a three.

MAGGIE & HAL: Really?

HAL: Why do we get a three? Is this a bit of racial profiling.

KELLY-ANN: We aren't allowed to do that. Let me put it this way. The only names we get are people somebody is already suspicious of, so, you know, you got to acknowledge that.

MAGGIE: Not that I know much but aren't most terrorists pretty young--

KELLY-ANN: When you look at them all together you see they come in all shapes and sizes--Israelis last year caught two grandmothers smuggling explosives in from Egypt.

ACT ONE; SCENE THREE

MAGGIE: So three is sort of a baseline ranking for anybody who comes to your attention?

KELLY-ANN: That's about it. Then you look for things unusual, you know, well those boxes I caught a glimpse of inside your rig. If I was doing a screening and I got the data that the subject was entering the country in an RV with a bunch of big cardboard boxes. I might get curious about them and run a DDC. Maybe a three plus.

MAGGIE: Oh those, things for my brother. He's building a beach house and--

KELLY-ANN: There you go 99.9 percent of the time, building supplies.

HAL: What's a DDC?

KELLY-ANN: Deep Data Check--a special, interactive program we use.

HAL: We were a little concerned that there might be a problem because we didn't declare them--the things for Maggie's brother-- at the border. I mean we probably were supposed to pay duty.

KELLY-ANN: These boys aren't interested in building supplies.

HAL: Drugs eh?

KELLY-ANN: Drugs they'd just be blocking the road North.

MAGGIE: Then what are they looking for?

KELLY-ANN: My guess it's got to do with all these pipeline blow-ups. Captain Ramirez let on they got a counter-terrorist team up from Mexico City. Otherwise he would have let us through in a flash.

[Maggie controls the urge to faint.]

HAL: A caravan of snowbirds wouldn't be involved in blowing up pipe-lines.

DUSTY: Be a perfect cover.

KELLY-ANN: There you go.

WAGONMASTER [O.S.]: Wagonmaster to Sheriff. What's your twenty?

> *[Kelly-Ann pulls a previously undisclosed walkie-talkie out of her fannie-pack.]*

KELLY-ANN: I'm back here relaxing with the Pauncho Villas.

WAGONMASTER [O.S.]: Kelly Jean, need you up front. There's been a change of plans. Captain Ramirez is here with some new folks and it seems that now he needs to follow customary procedure and inspect the RVs individually.

DUSTY: Customary, my you know what.

KELLY-ANN: I'm on my way. Ten-four.

> *[Back to]]*

See what I can do to hurry this along.

> *[To Dusty]*

See you back at the chuck wagon.

> *[She gives Dusty a big smack on the lips and exits.]*

DUSTY: I better get back to the rig and get ready to spread my cheeks when the Don Capitán comes calling.

HAL: They wouldn't.

DUSTY: Just kidding, just kidding...

> *[Dusty exits laughing.]*

MAGGIE: Do you still think everything is "cool", Hal?

HAL: The worst thing we can do is to get paranoid.

MAGGIE" Paranoid? We've just had a Homeland Security officer over for a beer, we are about to be searched by an anti-terrorist squad from Mexico City and we have-- Paranoid doesn't begin to describe how the prospect of spending the next umpteen years in a Mexican jail.

> *[Breaking down]*

Omigod! Omigod!

ACT ONE; SCENE THREE

[Hal goes to her; Maggie pushes him away.]

MAGGIE: The dream came back last night.

HAL: What?

MAGGIE" About my birth mother. I woke up screaming.

HAL; I'm sorry Maggie I--

MAGGIE; At first it was the same. She's lying on the ground covered in blood and I'm holding onto her dress fighting them off but as I'm being pulled away, I turn back and it's you on the ground staring back at me with dead eyes. You!

HAL; Mags ..it's going to be alright. This is coincidence, it has got to be.

[She won't let Hall touch her.]

MAGGIE: No it doesn't and you know it.

[Holds out a shaky hand.]

That's fear pure fear that I never wanted to feel again.

END OF ACT

ACT TWO; SCENE ONE
THE RV-LATER

Lights up: They wait. Maggie has changed into a tank top Hal is shirtless and sweating. He adjusts the vents on the AC.

HAL: Better?

MAGGIE: No.

WAGONMASTER [O.S.]: Listen up snowbirds. Two more to go so button up your rigs and be ready to roll.

MAGGIE: We're next.

HAL: We just have to keep our cool. Trust me.

MAGGIE: Trust you? A sick joke if there ever was one--
   [A KNOCK.]

INSPECTOR [O.S.]: Aduana.

MAGGIE: Si, me voy.

   [Hal, grabs a tee-shirt and pulls it on then seeing it has some anti-war slogan on it, rips it off and puts on another--this time backwards. Flustered, he reverses it as Maggie reaches for the door, then spots some magazines and stuffs them in a drawer before opening it.]

MAGGIE: Buenos días.

INSPECTOR [O.S.]: Buenos días señora, Inspector Hector Flores a sus ordenes.

MAGGIE: Margarita Lass, Inspector Flores, pasale.

   [The INSPECTOR enters. He is an unassuming looking man in his late twenties with a genial manner. He is dressed in a rayon guayabera and slacks. A badge on a lanyard dangles from his neck and a microphone receiver is fitted in his ear. The inspector references the caravan roster list fastened on a clipboard.]

ACT TWO; SCENE ONE

HAL: Hal Lass. Buenos Días Inspector.

INSPECTOR: Los dos hablán Español?

HAL: Mas o menos.

MAGGIE: Traduciré por él.

INSPECTOR *[Fluent]]:* No problem. You are from Berkeley, California?

MAGGIE: Yes...

INSPECTOR: We were neighbors. I lived in Milpitas.

HAL: No kidding.

INSPECTOR: I am not kidding. What is the purpose of your trip?

HAL: Vacation.

INSPECTOR: How long will you be in Mexico?

HAL: Four weeks.

INSPECTOR: Your passport please.

[Hal turns over his passport. The Inspector flips it open.]

INSPECTOR: You were born in Chicago, 1949?

HAL: Yes.

INSPECTOR: You ever go to Wrigley field?

HAL: Oh lots, I was a big Cubbies fan.

INSPECTOR: I like the Cubbies, always struggling, never winning. Like my country.

HAL: Mexico threw out Spain, then the French.

INSPECTOR: But against the U.S. no way.

HAL: "So far from God so close to the United States."

INSPECTOR: But what does that mean?

HAL: That, well, Mexico suffers from being so close to the United States.

INSPECTOR: Yes, but 'so far from God'. Why is Mexico so far from God?

HAL: Perhaps Diaz was coming from a Catholic perspective that Mexico, because of its pagan roots, is beyond the help of God -- the only force powerful enough to save them from being devoured by the United States.

INSPECTOR: I don't think God cares one way or the other. Do you?

HAL: No.

INSPECTOR: I think Diaz was drunk when he said it.

[The Inspector turns to Maggie. She has her passport ready.]

INSPECTOR *[Taking her passport]:* Thank you... You are a naturalized U.S. citizen Mrs. Lass. Do you have dual citizenship?

MAGGIE: Yes.

INSPECTOR: Your Mexican passport please.

[Maggie pulls it from her purse and turns it over. He opens it and speaks into his radio mike.]

INSPECTOR: Habla Inspector Flores.

RADIO [O.S.]: Digame Inspector.

INSPECTOR: Margarita Lass, nació Los Ocotes, Chiapas, 1957, domicilio Berkeley, California. Numéro del pasaporte, 187S9003.

MAGGIE: I entered Mexico on my U.S. passport.

INSPECTOR: National Bureau of Taxation has asked to be informed when a Mexican citizen of dual nationality enters the country. What is in those boxes?

HAL: A compostable toilet and an instant hot water heater.

MAGGIE: My brother is building a house and-

INSPECTOR: Your customs' receipts please.

HAL: Were we supposed to declare them?

[The Inspector answers with a look.]

MAGGIE: We were going to ask but they waved us through.

INSPECTOR: I assume you have brought other things for your relatives?

ACT TWO; SCENE ONE

MAGGIE: Well, yes but we mostly fly and--

INSPECTOR: You thought by road customs regulations would not apply?

MAGGIE: If we need to pay duty, we'd be glad to pay it now. Just tell us what we owe.

HAL: If it is allowed perhaps we could give you the money...

INSPECTOR: Are you offering me a mordita ?

MAGGIE: No, no, my husband--

HAL: You could give us a receipt if you like or, I could give you one...

INSPECTOR: Nobody pays duties. Mexicans want their government to wipe their culos for them but nobody wants to pay for the toilet paper...So far from God too close to Sam's Club. Verdad?

[Hal's and Maggie's genial laughs are cut short.]

INSPECTOR: Open those boxes for me please.

HAL: They're factory sealed. It will take some doing.

INSPECTOR: Would you like assistance?

HAL: No problem.

[Hal takes a tool kit from a drawer and pulls staples, removes bands, and layers of packing material. The RV gets cluttered. Maggie watches Hal intently while the Inspector thumbs through her passport,]

INSPECTOR: Berkeley's a good place to live, no?

MAGGIE: What? Oh, yes it is. Do you know it?

INSPECTOR: Do they still call it Beserkley?

MAGGIE: Some people do.

INSPECTOR: You are a professor?

MAGGIE: Yes.

INSPECTOR: What do you teach, Mrs. Lass; or is it Profesora Lass?

MAGGIE: Whichever you prefer. I teach global studies. It's part of the political science department.

INSPECTOR *[Referring to her passport.]:* ...Chile, Kenya, India, Venezuela. You travel a lot?

MAGGIE: Conferences mostly.

INSPECTOR: About what?

MAGGIE: Different subjects related to my field.

INSPECTOR: For example?

MAGGIE: Well, I gave a paper at the international symposium on African women's health in Nairobi last year on international programs to eradicate female circumcision.

INSPECTOR: Why is that your business?

MAGGIE: Female genital mutilation is an act of torture and as such, it is everyone's business.

INSPECTOR: And Venezuela, the purpose of your visit?

MAGGIE: A conference on gender equity.

INSPECTOR: Did you meet President Chavez?

MAGGIE: He addressed the plenary session. Why is this relevant?

INSPECTOR: Relevant to what?

MAGGIE: A customs inspection.

INSPECTOR: Why do you think this is a customs inspection?

MAGGIE: Then what is its purpose?

INSPECTOR: La paz y seguridad de México, profesora.

[Hal pulls the cover off the box exposing the toilet. The Inspector walks over and pulls out the invoice.]

INSPECTOR: Sixteen hundred and seventy-four dollars. Does it brush your teeth?

HAL: It's Consumer Reports top pick in the waterless toilet category.

INSPECTOR: My mother says when she crossed over what

ACT TWO; SCENE ONE

she loved the most about El Norte were the flush toilets. You couldn't give her one of these.

[The Inspector dumps the toilet out of its box and searches through the packing, then moves on to other things.]

INSPECTOR: When we lived on the other side it was bring us this, bring us that. Pinche relatives always have their hands out, true?

MAGGIE: My brother doesn't, inspector.

INSPECTOR: You are a lucky chicana, profesora, and unique.

MAGGIE: Do you mind my asking why you moved to Mexico?

INSPECTOR: My father got deported so the family went with him.

MAGGIE: I'm sorry, it's unconscionable--

INSPECTOR: No need to apologize; it was a blessing. I went back to college, got my degree. I am happy to be in my own country that does not disrespect my family.

MAGGIE: I can certainly understand that.

INSPECTOR: And when was it you crossed over?

MAGGIE: I was adopted as an infant.

INSPECTOR: Yes, here it is June 10, 1960. We crossed paths. How do you find your new country, Profesora?

MAGGIE: It has its problems.

INSPECTOR *[Turning to Hal.]:* Mr. Lass, you are journalist?

HAL: Retired.

INSPECTOR: Are you famous?

HAL: No. I worked for a university alumni magazine.

INSPECTOR: Did you publish the profesora's papers?

HAL: My specialty was rich alumni.

[The Inspector pulls open the drawers and finds the stack of magazines Maggie stuffed in one of them. A copy of the AARP magazine is on the top. He picks it up.]

INSPECTOR: My papí gets this.

HAL: He's retired?

INSPECTOR; Twenty-six years he worked for Ford in Milpitas then eight more in Monterey. Now he is everyday in his garage rebuilding muscle cars....My mother complains but he won't stop.

HAL: He must enjoy it.

INSPECTOR: He loves the money. Sells them in Dallas to old white guys. You want I'll get you a good deal. Right now he's doing a 1973 Barracuda, eight cylinder, 360 block, 727 trans?

HAL: No thanks. I'm not much of a car person.

INSPECTOR: Too bad.

[He notices the other magazines and checks them out: Amnesty International, Human Rights Watch, The Nation.]

INSPECTOR: How do you pass your retirement, Mr. Lass?

HAL: I read, go to films, the gym--sometimes. Meet friends for coffee. I'm not ambitious like your father.

INSPECTOR: You have a favorite cafe to meet your friends, Mr. Lass?

HAL: Not really.

INSPECTOR: What are the names of the cafes you go to, please?

HAL: Cafe Med that's on Telegraph--maybe you know it.... Rigolettos. Red Dog Books. You can read their books all day for the price of a cup of coffee.

INSPECTOR: Do you know Cafe Paloma?

HAL: Sure, it's been in Berkeley longer than we have.

INSPECTOR: Do you go there?

HAL: Not much. Their coffee isn't very good.

INSPECTOR: Their free internet is very popular.

HAL: I wouldn't know.

ACT TWO; SCENE ONE

INSPECTOR: You'd rather talk with your friends?

HAL: Talk, read a book, people watch.-

INSPECTOR: Jorge Calderón? Jose Rivera? Do you have coffee with them when you go to Cafe Paloma?

HAL: Those names aren't familiar.

INSPECTOR: Are you sure?

HAL: Perhaps I'd recognize them if I saw them. When you are retired there are a number of people you cross paths with, some daily, whose names you never know. I think of them as my ghost friends.

INSPECTOR *[Into his microphone]*: Habla Flores...

RADIO [O.S.]: A sus ordenes Inspector.

INSPECTOR: Por favor, llevame los fotos de los personas de interés.

RADIO [O.S.]: ¿A donde?

INSPECTOR: Vehiculo cinco.

[Hal and Maggie are not pleased.]

INSPECTOR: Tell me about your ghost friends.

[As Hal prattles on, the Inspector continues searching the RV. Hal follows him about the camper trying to distract him.]

HAL: Lets see...There's a man, about my age, actually a bit older with a slight limp, who takes the same route for his morning walk as I do except in the opposite direction. I give him a wave and he tips his cap when we pass. When I don't see him, I'm genuinely concerned--worried he's had a stroke and been bundled off to some home. Then there are those in the market and the regulars at the film archive seniors' matinee. We banter back and forth about the price of fruit or the last film we saw but never further intruding on each others' lives. They say at my age, the idea of new intimacy is an unsettling proposition.

[The Inspector's search grows increasingly intrusive: he finds Maggie's toilet kit and empties it checking the labels on pill bottles.]

HAL: I'm boring you. What you want to know about are the people I meet in cafes. Frankly, I mostly keep to myself unless there is no alternative but to share a table and conversation ensues. Sometimes I enjoy it but I always have an ear out for the 'Droners' who babble interminably about their particular obsession more often than not a conspiracy- -Nine-Eleven the favorite by far. They've ruined many a good coffee house for me. Them and the clickety-click of laptop keys are enough to give anybody a migraine. But among all the humans I encounter in my quotidian existence, I can count people who I know by name on one hand. So that's a long way of saying: I may have met your friends, even shared a table with them at Cafe Paloma, if that is where they go, but I most definitely don't know your friends by name.

INSPECTOR: Oh they aren't my friends, Mr. Lass. They are cabrónes. You know what a cabrón is Mr. Lass?

HAL: Basically an asshole.

INSPECTOR: You do know some Spanish.

[A Knock. Kelly-Ann enters with a folder.]

KELLY-ANN: Your Sergeant asked me to bring you these...

INSPECTOR: Thank you Agent Fuerst. Please stay.

[The Inspector opens the folder and looks through the collection of wanted circulars as the conversation continues.]

KELLY-ANN: How you folks doing?

MAGGIE: It seems we've created a problem not declaring the plumbing fixtures we're bringing my brother.

ACT TWO; SCENE ONE

INSPECTOR: I grew up next to the Lass's or close. We may have even walked by each other, tipped our caps, exchanged a nod.

KELLY-ANN: You all must have a lot to talk about.

INSPECTOR: Very true. It seems Mr. Lass takes his coffee at the cafe where two of our people of interest take advantage of the free Wi-Fi. But Mr. Lass says he doesn't know them, or he maybe knew them but not as Jorge Calderón and Jose Rivera. What names do you maybe know them by?

HAL: I have no idea if I know them by any name. I don't even know what they look like.

[To Kelly-Ann]

Cafe Paloma is a popular cafe and you often have to share a table if you want a seat, which is why I rarely go there.

[The Inspector pulls two circulars out of the folder and hands them to Hal.]

INSPECTOR: You recognize them, Mr. Lass?

[Hal looks and hands them back.]

HAL: They don't look familiar. It is certainly possible I might have had an exchange with one or the other or sat at the same table, but I really couldn't say.

INSPECTOR" So when you possibly shared a table with Jorge Calderón and Jose Rivera, whose names you don't know, what possibly did you discuss?

HAL: I don't know whether I shared a table so I don't know what we talked about.

INSPECTOR: Possibly you talked about blowing up things. Pipelines?

HAL: No, I would definitely remember that.

[The Inspector nods to the magazines.]

INSPECTOR: You haven't read about it in your papers, not in

Amnesty International, Human Rights Watch, The Nation , how these pinche cabrónes are blowing up Mexico's pipelines?

HAL: I thought you meant...Yes I have read about it in a number of papers.

INSPECTOR: What did you think I meant?

HAL *[Flustered]:* Well, whether I heard any discussion of it in Berkeley--and I haven't.

INSPECTOR: And if you heard some cabrónes making plans to blow up my country's pipelines you would report it?

HAL: Absolutely, to the appropriate authority.

INSPECTOR: But you didn't hear anybody talking about blowing up pipelines?

HAL: I answered that.

INSPECTOR: I forget your answer?

HAL: No.

INSPECTOR: No, you didn't hear Jose Rivera and Jorge Calderón talk about blowing up pipelines or "No" you won't answer my question again?

HAL: I don't know the two men whose pictures you showed me; consequently, I have never heard them discuss blowing up pipelines.

INSPECTOR: You heard others discuss it?

HAL: No.

INSPECTOR: But you knew about it?

HAL: I read about it in the newspapers or heard on the radio.

INSPECTOR: But you didn't discuss it with your friends at Cafe Paloma?

HAL: Not that I remember--not with those two in your pictures.

INSPECTOR: Do you remember whether they asked you to carry explosives with you to Mexico?

ACT TWO; SCENE ONE

HAL: No. Most definitely.

INSPECTOR: No they didn't ask or no, you don't remember?

MAGGIE: Inspector, my husband has answered your questions. He has said he doesn't know the two men. And he has never been asked to bring explosives to Mexico.

INSPECTOR: How about you, profesora. Did Jose Rivera or Jorge Calderón ask you to bring explosives to Mexico?

MAGGIE: I'm not acquainted with either man but neither I nor my husband know about nor do we support sabotage in Mexico or anywhere else.

INSPECTOR: Yes, I believe that you don't. But your husband, maybe he thinks it is good that these pinche cabrónes are blowing up our pipelines?

[Hal steps in cutting off Maggie.]

HAL: Sabotage eh, pull out the black cat?-- That's what they used to say--the early anarchists--time for the Black Cat. Did you know the word sabotage comes from the French word "sabot" which were the wood shoes worn by 19th Century French workers? When the mill owners would speed up the machines beyond endurance the workers would throw their sabots into the gears to stop them--essentially a worker decreed coffee break.

INSPECTOR: I am not asking you about France.

HAL: I was giving some background. Sabotage, as a tactic, had some success particularly at the beginning of the industrial revolution but, when it was later elevated to a strategy, it failed miserably. In the U.S. it had a lot to do with the destruction of the IWW, in Mexico, the destruction of the Magón brothers' Liberal Party.

[The Inspector continues tearing apart the RV. Sticking his nose in everything.]

HAL: It is my belief, Inspector, and history bears this out. Inspector--this is important--that sabotage more often than not is carried out by agent-provocateurs to discredit people's movements.

INSPECTOR: The ceiling from here to the back is lower?

KELLY-ANN: That's the design of this model they provide more insulation for the living section.

[Inspector takes a closer look. Reaching over his head. We see his equipment belt where he carries, an automatic, cuffs, flashlight and electric screwdriver. Hal continues as the Inspector removes the screws that hold the panel in place.]

HAL: So, inspector, if your alleged saboteurs approached me with some cockamamie plan of blowing up pipelines I would tell them what I have just related to you and then, to be safe, tell my lawyer that I may have been approached by police agents and put it in her hands...But no-one approached me. The panel clatters to the floor and insulation tumbles out covering the Inspector.

INSPECTOR: You are right, Agent Fuerst, insulation.

KELLY-ANN: Be a damn fool place to put explosives probably gets hot enough in there to set them off.

[The RV is now a total disaster zone. The inspector uses his mag-lite to examine the space.]

HAL: Is it all right to clean up now?

INSPECTOR *[Into his radio]:* Habla Flores

RADIO [O.S.]: Digame Inspector.

INSPECTOR: Por favor, quiero Sargento Martinez y sus perros vienen a vehículo cinco.

RADIO: Claro, Inspector.

MAGGIE: Dogs?

INSPECTOR: A gift, from your Homeland Security: fruit sniffing

ACT TWO; SCENE ONE

beagles retrained to sniff explosives. Do you have something you'd like to tell me profesora?

MAGGIE: Yes, you've made a mess of our camper for no good reason and I hope you plan to clean it up.

[The Inspector and Maggie have a stare down for a beat broken by dogs YAPPING.]

RADIO [O.S.]: Estoy afuera Inspector.

INSPECTOR: Andale. Sargento.

[Sounds of the dogs scurrying beneath the RV.]

MAGGIE: This is just- just outrageous.

[The Inspector exits.]

HAL: Does this happen a lot?

KELLY-ANN: Well I couldn't say--

[Pointing to the magazines strewn on the futon]

They're just the ones we're told to be on the look out for...

[The Inspector returns.]

INSPECTOR: Those dogs should stick to fruit.

[Into his microphone]

Habla Flores.

RADIO [O.S.]: A sus ordenes Inspector

INSPECTOR: Quiero que quede vehículo cinco, placa de California DX773C y darle el Full Monte.

RADIO [O.S.]: Momento.

HAL: What did he say? What's that about Full Monte?

KELLY-ANN: Like the movie. They strip it down to the axles.

[Hal and Maggie look like they are going to piss themselves.]

MAGGIE: This is nothing but harassment.

INSPECTOR: Profesora, why would I want to harass you?

MAGGIE: Because--because your father was deported -unjustly and a...

INSPECTOR: You offered me a bribe? You think perhaps I was insulted? I assure you it is normal.

[To Kelly-Ann]]

What do you think, Agent Fuerst. Would Homeland Security think I am harassing the profesora and Mr. Lass?

KELLY-ANN: I'm not a field agent, Inspector, and on vacation at that, but you haven't found anything.

INSPECTOR: True, but I think we will, don't you Mr. Lass? I think now is your opportunity to tell us, take the responsibility so that your wife is not involved.

HAL

I--

[Hal opens his mouth to confess; Maggie interrupts.]

MAGGIE: The only way explosives or anything else will be found in our RV, Inspector is if somebody else put them there without our knowledge.

RADIO [O.S.]: Inspector Flores

INSPECTOR: Digame.

RADIO [O.S.]: Inspector, the captain has received orders that we should precede immediately to back-up a roadblock on Route Sixty, South of Torréon.

INSPECTOR: Fine but I want to detain this RV for a full inspection.

RADIO [O.S.]: Momento...

CAPTAIN [O.S.]: Capitán Maceas, Inspector. Digame.

INSPECTOR: I have reason to believe these people in vehicle five are EPR.

CAPTAIN: They are Yanqui jubilados, no?

INSPECTOR: The husband admits to frequenting Cafe Paloma in Berkeley, California from which EPR members communicate over the internet.

CAPTAINL And?

ACT TWO; SCENE ONE

INSPECTOR: They have radical publications in their vehicle and--

CAPTAIN: What did the dogs find?

INSPECTOR: Those dogs couldn't find their own culos.

CAPTAIN: And your search of the vehicle you found?

INSPECTOR: Radical publications and they also avoided declaring construction material they were bringing--

CAPTAIN: I have my orders inspector. I don't want to waste more time here.

INSPECTOR: But Captain -Captain?

[Disgusted the Inspector clicks off.]

INSPECTOR *[To Hal]:* You are very lucky.

[Inspector turns to leave.]

HAL: Could we have our passports please?

[Reluctantly he hands them to Hal.[

INSPECTOR: Hasta pronto.

[The Inspector exits.]

KELLY-ANN: He left you with a mess.

HAL: He didn't like us--that's for sure.

KELLY-ANN: Well, I better run along--Dusty's been into the beers so I'm the designated driver.

[She opens the door and then turns around.]

KELLY-ANN: I don't know what you folks are up to but you take good care 'cause the Mexicans--and I love 'em to death--don't like it when other people get in their business anymore than we do...

[Kelly-Ann exits and for Hal and Maggie absolute relief.]

HAL: I almost pissed myself

MAGGIE: They know.

HAL: If they knew, we'd have been arrested. I grant you that we set some bells off: Luciano's stuff didn't help and those magazines--I should have thought of that.

MAGGIE: Next time your smuggling guns I'll run out and buy copies of 'People' for the trip.

HAL: You were tough Mags. I was ready to give it up and you just got right in his face--

MAGGIE: Desperate. I don't know why we weren't arrested but they know, I can feel it. Kelly-Ann as much as said it.

HAL: Maggie, if they know they would have busted us before we left Berkeley or when we crossed at Nogales.

MAGGIE: How did we wind up cheek to jowl with Homeland Security?

HAL: Coincidence. If she's tracking us would she introduce herself as a Homeland Security agent?

MAGGIE: They're waiting to see who you bring them to.

HAL: Then why make a big fuss here? To alert us? We got stopped at a roadblock by Dudley-Do-Right who sees we're from Berkeley and busts our chops. He doesn't believe I had anything to do with the pipeline sabotage --and I don't--that's the EPR. We're carrying guns not explosives. That's why the dogs didn't smell anything.

MAGGIE: Those pictures he showed you, do you know them?

HAL: No- at least not to speak to.

MAGGIE: What!

HAL: I think, Jaime pointed one of them out once in the Berkeley Bowl. It may not be him, probably not.

MAGGIE: I'll call Luciano. He knows people--

HAL: Maggie we'll be in the Guadalajara RV park tomorrow night. If you're right, they'll be watching me. I'll take the RV into the city. While they're following me, you take a cab to the airport and catch a plane--there's one leaving to San Francisco or LA almost every hour. I'll say we had a family emergency.

MAGGIE: They won't believe you.

ACT TWO; SCENE ONE

HAL: What can they do about it?

MAGGIE: Inside a Mexican jail, a lot. We have to get a lawyer, find some doctors to say you've had a--

HAL: Maggie, Mags, you have to work with me, especially they're tracking us. I'm not operating on my own. We have a plan in place.

MAGGIE: Oh Hal....

HAL: You think I'm nuts, don't you?

MAGGIE: Not nuts , suicidal.

HAL: I'm alive again Mags, alive! When that inspector was going at me I was scared, but not for a moment did I regret bringing guns only that I involved you.

MAGGIE: They'll kill you Hal.

HAL: Not me I'm the cautious type...

MAGGIE: You don't have to go through with this...They'll be watching the RV--We'll just leave it at the RV park and fly home. We'll say the guns were planted.

HAL: A street corner preacher with stains on my pants---you nailed me. That's what I had become and I didn't like it anymore than anybody else. Mags, I know you think it's foolish, useless--

MAGGIE: These groups live in the damn jungle. You haven't been camping since we moved to California,

HAL: I have too--sure I have. I took Frida and her friend camping. Remember?

MAGGIE: To the Berkeley city camp. Hal, you're sixty years old for go sakes. You have bunions!

HAL: I promise I won't go on any foot patrols....

MAGGIE: I can't join you Hal. I can't.

HAL: Maggie, I'm going to get you out of here. No worries.

MAGGIE: And after you deliver them, what are you going to do?

HAL: I haven't thought that far ahead.

MAGGIE: I want you to come home to me.

HAL: I love you. I always have.

>*[Hal reaches out, touching Maggie. They embrace. A C&W road tune plays over the CB.]*

WAGONMASTER [O.S.]: Snowbirds, lock and load. We're good to go. Vehicle One...

FADE TO BLACK

ACT TWO; SCENE ONE

EPILOGUE

Lights Up.
Stage Left. Maggie, looking professorial, stands behind her office desk, She puts her lecture notes in her briefcase, closes it, and looks up at the audience.

MAGGIE: I made it home from Guadalajara then I waited... Weeks turned into months. Half the time I was afraid he was dead the other half I wanted to kill the crazy bastard.

[Fighting her emotions]

That Spring I was walking across campus and a young man addressed me in Spanish, "Compañera, please sit down." He said it was his duty to inform me, that "Compañero Pauncho died heroically defending a safe house during a raid by para-militaries. ...He handed me Hal's watch...

Hard times...Two years this November.

Now, when I think about Hal, I force myself to think back to when I first laid eyes on him, cutting across Mass Ave, his army surplus jacket billowing out behind him, hell-bent on changing the world.

[Maggie, collects herself... A bell RINGS. She checks the time. She is wearing Hal's watch.]

MAGGIE: Class.

[Maggie gathers her belonging off her desk and exits.]

END OF PLAY

BIG MONEY

.SCENES

Act One

Scene One: Green Room
Scene Two: Sam and Karen's loft - later
Scene Three: Zeke's Outdoor Dining Deck
Scene Four: Loft - later
Scene Five: Austin; Private airport lounge -- A month later

Act Two

Scene One: Loft
Scene Two: Sam's office - Two months later
Scene Three: Loft - Months later
Scene Four: Sam's office
Scene Five: Loft - days later
Scene Six: Eric's house - later
Scene Seven: Loft - later

CAST

Sam Garcia: mid-thirties, Foundation director.
Karen Michaels: mid-thirties, Marine biologist; Sam's partner
Eric Deveraux: forties, Venture capitalist

BIG MONEY

ACT ONE; SCENE ONE
GREEN ROOM

A video highlighting the Environmental Justice Movement plays as Sam speaks. The video includes images of Sam: speaking at an Earth Day Rally; being arrested at a sit-ins; leading a demonstration at a petrochemical refinery.

SAM [O.S.]...Last year Matrix Foundation made environmental justice grants to a hundred and forty-six organizations in 20 states and six countries. It is your generosity that made this possible. So a big shout-out to all of you for your time, your resources, your commitment but most of all to a shared vision of a possible planet where environmental justice and social equality rules.

[Applause dies. Lights up on a modest green room in a downtown hotel. A pair of motorcycle helmets are slung across the mini-bar.]

[Stage Right. Sam Garcia, who we recognize from the video, enters with Karen Michaels. They are a confident, fit couple in their mid-thirties. Sam walks with a slight limp.]

SAM: Did you see anybody that might be him?

KAREN: There's a skinny guy, with a blingy wristwatch and cashmere blazer sitting next to Carl Tompkins.

SAM: Probably him.

KAREN: You want me to bring him back for you?

SAM: I'll go out in a minute. How did you know it was cashmere?

KAREN: It went baa.

[Sam, pulls a beer out of the mini-bar and collapses onto the couch, tired.]

ACT ONE; SCENE ONE

SAM: I'm obsessed with money.

[Karen joins Sam on the couch and massages his neck.]

KAREN: Isn't it an occupational hazard of foundation directors?

SAM *[Hamming]:* Save me before I ask again!

KAREN: You should get the board to hire a full time fund raiser.

SAM: Fat chance. They're in a leaner meaner mode.

KAREN: Maybe you should get a little pushy?

SAM: I have.

[Sam reaches behind him and pulls Karen in to his lap.]

SAM: Hey, you want to shoot some pool later?

KAREN: Yeah, let's go to La Bomba but not too late. I need to get home to check on something.

[Karen helps herself to his beer.]

SAM: What?

KAREN: You'll find out.

[Some smooching....]

[Stage Left. ERIC DEVERAUX, a youthful and greyhound sleek enters.]

ERIC: Uh, excuse me.

[Sam is up and reaching for Eric's hand. Karen gets her public face on.]

SAM: Sam Garcia, you must be Eric Deveraux.

ERIC: Last time I checked.

SAM: Thanks so much for coming. My partner, Karen Michaels.

KAREN: Great to meet you, Eric. Sam was just asking if you were here.

SAM: I wanted to thank you in person. We get a hundred, two hundred, occasionally a thousand dollar donations unsolicited but $60,000.--Never. It didn't make my week. It made my year.

ERIC: It was a pleasure to write the check. Matrix Foundation is a super organization. I've been going around to a few of these events of local foundations trying to find one that inspired me and you guys really distinguished yourself from the pack.

SAM: Our good fortune.

ERIC: Your good works and by the way, loved your talk. It cleared up some questions I had.

SAM: Can I ask you what questions?

ERIC: Defining environmental justice. I know you fund good works and all, but the vision behind them, which you framed as part of an historical legacy that goes back to the civil rights movement and Martin Luther King, that nailed it for me. And that lady before you--

SAM: Margaret Johnson?

ERIC: What a story. Did you see that movie Erin Brocovich?

SAM: Sure.

ERIC: Her story reminded me of that but worse. It's effing outrageous.

SAM: It's business as usual in the petrochemical industry--to this day.

ERIC: It was so clear from what the lady was saying that Matrix coming along was the tipping point to their success.

SAM: She's a remarkable women. She organized the group door-to-door, church to church, while raising six kids and working full time as a school custodian.

ERIC: Of all the groups on the Matrix web-site, my favorite are those medical students in Louisiana. I checked out their You Tube video.

SAM: A bunch of them just got busted for setting up their medical van outside the Balero Chemical refinery to test the levels of arsenic, lead and cyanide in the workers' blood.

ACT ONE; SCENE ONE

The refinery manager swore out a warrant for trespassing. They arrested five and impounded their medical van with all their equipment. They e-mailed us this morning for an emergency grant to get their van out of the impound lot. Thanks to your donation we could do it.

ERIC: You know the president of a corporation like that has to know he's poisoning his own people. How does he sleep at night?

SAM: Not well after the video of the bust was featured state-wide on the 6 o'clock news.

ERIC: I just sent Senator Murray's campaign committee a check. I should ask her to look into the situation down there.

SAM: It wouldn't hurt.

ERIC: You got it.

KAREN: Eric, could I get you a beer or something?

ERIC: I don't want to monopolize the rest of your evening, it looked like you two had other plans.

KAREN: No, no why don't you hang.

SAM: Hey, you can't donate $60,000 to Matrix and not even have a beer with us.

KAREN: I'll snag some finger food.

ERIC: You know, if you can find a Red Bull.

KAREN: You got it.

ERIC: I know it's terrible for you but-

KAREN: No worries, Sam often comes home with Red Bull on his breath. Later guys.

[Karen Exits]

SAM: Sit down and relax.

[Sitting down, Sam guides his left leg a bit with his hands.]

SAM: I was wondering how you first heard of Matrix?

ERIC: I read a story in an airline magazine about the group that organizes community gardens in LA.

SAM: You're talking about Eden Gardens in Watts?

ERIC: Right.

SAM: "Build a garden; feed a neighborhood; create a community."

ERIC: You were their original funder?

SAM: Matrix and the Semillas Foundation. They're starting a community garden in East Palo Alto.

ERIC: That's right next door to me. I got a couple of acres around my house in Atherton. Maybe they'd like to build a garden there.

SAM: Their projects are based on unused land in their own communities but I'm sure they'd give you advice and I know in LA they freelance their services as gardeners.

ERIC: Hey that's an idea. But if I could be of any help-- a fund raiser at the house or something-

SAM: Fantastic. With your permission I'll give Mario Garza--he runs the project--your e-mail.

ERIC: Give him my cell number.

SAM: Cool. He's an interesting dude. He started gardening when he was doing ten in Folsom for armed robbery. It turned his life around. He'll have you on his board before you can blink.

ERIC: You know, Sam, I keep being struck by similarities in what we do.

SAM: How do you mean?.

ERIC: Well, we both invest in start-ups and success is our goal.

SAM: In a sense, but we measure success differently.

ERIC: How's that?

SAM: For the environmental justice movement success is measured in large part by overcoming social inequalities and environmental degradation of the planet. For venture

ACT ONE; SCENE ONE

capitalism, capitalism in general, success is measured by maximizing profit which invariably increases social inequalities.

ERIC: What about investing in biotechnology--you can make money as well as benefit humanity?

SAM: Depends on who has access to the results--Steve Jobs gets a new pancreas--and there's nothing wrong with that--but what about the farm worker who needs another pancreas because of pesticide poisoning--no way.

ERIC: The hope is that eventually they'll be available to everyone.

SAM: The pancreas trickle-down theory?

ERIC: Well, look at me. I'm a venture-capitalist who has made a lot of money, now I'm ready to give back-- if it wasn't for capitalism I wouldn't have the money and you wouldn't be talking to me, am I right?

SAM: 60K is a good conversation starter, I'll give you that. I spend eighty percent of my time trying to convince folks with money to give it to us.

ERIC: You have me reaching for my wallet.

SAM: Eric, I took a look at your web-site and I was blown away. I was curious how you got started?

ERIC: It's not real interesting--take my word for it.

SAM: Try me.

ERIC: Well, let's see...I went to business college--quit after a semester. Bored the shit out of me. My old man--he had Semper-Fi tattooed on his eyeballs--wanted me in the Marines--no way. I left home and lived in my car until I talked my way into the mail room at Goldman-Sachs. I spent months studying annual reports--don't think I slept more than three hours a night-- and when I figured out about the direction of a few companies I passed the info on to one of the equity partners, who I was scoring pot for. They panned out, I was made a broker trainee and I was on my way.

SAM: How long were you at Goldman-Sachs?

ERIC: Ten years, about. I got bored, quit, and began looking for start-ups. I invested in a small B2B, that caught on. Microsoft bought us out for thirty million. I leveraged my share, pulled together a capital pool of five hundred million and set up shop in Silicon Gulch. Every I/T geek with a brilliant idea knocked on my door. Out of twelve companies I backed, six went belly-up, three paid back their investment and a little more and three paid off big time. So here I am with a shit-load of money and wondering what to do with the rest of my life.

SAM: You want to get out of investing?

ERIC: No, but making money doesn't do it for me anymore. I grew up in public housing in South Boston Mom was a nurse's aide; my old man worked construction--when he worked. My goal was to get rich--capital R and I was lucky, blessed or both. I've built my house, bought a Lamborghini, bought a Ferrari, now I drive a Tesla. Last year I went around the world on a private jet tour-- five stars all the way. I saw Machu Pichu under a full moon, we had a ten course meal at the Taj Mahal catered by the top chef in India, climbed the pyramids at Luxor, the best was a four day photo safari in the Serengeti--I have the photos I shot up on my web-site-- But, you know, how many times can you chow down a five star Micheline meal before the thought doesn't occur to you; 'Is this all?' The other day I opened my top drawer looking for some nail clippers and it's stuffed with Rolexes and Breitlings that I never wore more than once. Sam, I turn fifty next year. Half-a-century and I want to know what good can I

ACT ONE; SCENE ONE

do?... Sam, I'm asking?

SAM: Eric, you and other donors totally underestimate the significance of their support. To me it's like hello? Your 60k donation will fund a half dozen environmental Sprout Grants: A res in South Dakota will be able to fund a campaign for federal and state monies to install sewer lines. An anti-fracking campaign in the coal mining region of western Pennsylvania will get a full time organizer. An anti-pcb landfill movement will get seed money for a campaign to put an initiative on the state ballot, an anti hilltop removal project in West Virginia will get funding to hire a lawyer, a community garden will be funded at the largest public high school in Los Angeles. And, as I told you, those medical students in Louisiana's cancer alley will get their medical van back. So my answer is, first of all, appreciate all the good that you are doing. I and the folks I mentioned sure the fuck do.

ERIC: Sam, I hear what you're saying but still-

SAM: Donors, particularly those that are financially well-off, have this idea that to be really pure they should give everything away and go around dressed in a garbage bag and flip-flops--no really--I've had people tell me that--they wished they were strong enough to give everything away. I call it the Dali Lama complex, who actually lives quite decently.

ERIC: No, I hear you.

SAM: There's nothing wrong with being wealthy. What's wrong is social injustice. Supporting and participating in the fight against it puts you on the side of the angels.

ERIC: I'll check in the mirror tomorrow and let you know if I've grown wings.

SAM: I think what you're saying is donating money is not enough. You'd like to get more involved?

ERIC: Yeah...You nailed it.

SAM: Let's talk about it. But first I need another beer. You sure you don't want one?

[Sam starts to get up, then stumbles.]

ERIC: Rest that leg.

[Eric gets the beer for Sam.]

ERIC: My assistant showed me a video she found of the boarding of that Japanese whaling ship-- That was some beating you took. Was the girl who whacked that guy with a pole--

SAM: Karen.

ERIC: That took some cajones. Both of you.

SAM: It didn't seem so at the time--we just did it.

ERIC: So, how'd you get involved in all this?

SAM: In my blood. My dad worked as an union organizer for the United Farm Workers Union, my mom too.

ERIC: Did they know Caesar Chavez?

SAM: He was my dad's mentor.

ERIC: Wow! Caesar Chavez is a hero of mine. How'd you end up fighting whalers?

SAM: My Dad's brother was a longshoreman in Oregon. During high school and college he got me on as a deckhand with the salmon fleet. It was when issues about overfishing were emerging and I got involved in that and I just liked being out on the water. I transferred from college to the Merchant Marine Academy, got by mate's license and signed on with the Good Shepherd.

ERIC: Your parents must be proud of you.

SAM: My dad would've preferred I went into the union movement but they've been supportive.

ERIC: Do you still have relatives in Mexico?

SAM: Never did. My mother's from Brooklyn and the Garcia's

ACT ONE; SCENE ONE

were Californians before it was California. My grandfather found a deed from the Spanish Viceroy to my great, great, great grandfather for a thousand acres in the Central Valley.

ERIC: Any of it still in the family?

SAM: No such luck. Most of it is now downtown Merced.

ERIC: So, how'd you get from fighting whalers to running Matrix?

SAM: My leg was too messed up to pass the physical to go back to sea so I went to work with the national organization.

ERIC: How long did you do that?

SAM: Too long. I thought I was going to be involved in policy but I was pretty much relegated to telling war stories and giving pitches. So when Katrina hit I took a leave of absence and went. I got involved in rebuilding housing in the lower Ninth. Matrix gave us some seed money and when their director quit they offered me the job.

ERIC: They must feel lucky to have you.

SAM: I hope so... Eric, do you mind if I bend your ear for a minute?

ERIC: I'm listening.

SAM: A strategic goal of Matrix is expanding our base of donors. Right now major donors cover approximately fifty percent of our budget. I have to spend most of my time beating the bushes to find the other half. The Gulch is a place were we have very few contacts and I was hoping that--

ERIC: Off the top I can think of maybe...yeah four, five guys I've been on deals with that might be interested in making a contribution to Matrix. A lot can be said about The Gulch and much of it not very complimentary but we're result oriented--and Matrix gets results. I'll set up a meet.

SAM: Fantastic. Sometimes it works better to have an informal gathering, I could give a five minute spiel, hand out our annual report and answer questions.

ERIC *[Checking his iPhone]]:* How about a lunch at Zeke's... Next Thursday?

SAM *[checking his iPhone]:* ...Perfect--Maybe before you could brief me on who's coming?

ERIC: You got it. We'll wait until then to formally announce that the 60K I gave to Matrix will be an annual donation.

SAM: Annual! This is fantastic Eric.

ERIC: Isn't that what you were hinting at?

SAM: Well-

ERIC: So I made it easy for you.

SAM: Thank you Eric thank you. I really didn't mean to pitch you to make--

ERIC: Sure you did, guy, and it gives me great pleasure to oblige.

BLACK OUT

ACT ONE; SCENE TWO
SAM AND KAREN'S LOFT-LATER

Sparsely furnished. An iconic UFW Boycott Grapes and an anti-whaling poster are on a wall. A large photo of Karen and Sam aboard the anti-whaling ship, The Good Shepherd sits on a counter. Up stage a bay window looks out over the city.]

Lights up. Discarded motorcycle helmets, jackets, and clothes around the bed where Karen and Sam lie entangled with each other. Karen slips out of bed, pulls on a bathrobe and walks over to the kitchen area, opens a cabinet and removes a drugstore pregnancy kit with the test stick in it. Sam joins her.

SAM: Is that?

[As she pulls the stick out.]

KAREN: Surprise.

SAM: Blue's positive?

KAREN: Yeah.

[He hugs her, ecstatic.]

SAM: Fantastic!

KAREN: Sam, these test kits aren't totally reliable.

[Sam reads from the box of the pregnancy kit.]

SAM: ...Ninety six percent accurate. I'll take those odds

KAREN: I'm over a month late.

SAM: This is so cool.

KAREN: Did you always want to have children?

SAM: I don't think I ever thought about not having kids.

KAREN: I know we decided, but it scares me a little.

SAM: Giving birth?

KAREN: Not so much; caring for them--

SAM: Nothing to it. You change their diapers, stick a bottle in their mouths and sing them a song when they cry.

KAREN: I wish I came from a big family.

SAM: We'll make our own.

KAREN: Whoa, one child maybe two.

SAM: Two is fine.

KAREN: Let's see how it goes with one.

SAM: What if it's twins?

KAREN: I don't want to even think about that.

SAM: Do you have any cravings?

> *[Karen separates from Sam and opens the refrigerator.]*

KAREN: Food, I'm starved. Shit. What if I'm eating for three.

> *[They scrounge through a week's worth of take-away leftovers, feeding themselves and each other as the conversation continues.]*

KAREN: Mmm. It's so great about that guy--

SAM: He's a foundation director's wet dream.

KAREN: Oh, I thought I was...

SAM: You're my own private wet dream come true.

KAREN: That's better.

> *[She gives him a kiss.]*

SAM: What did you think of him?

KAREN: 60K-you can't do any better than that.

SAM: You didn't like him?

KAREN: He seemed nice enough; he's just not someone I'd hang with.

SAM: He's from the business world, it's a different culture.

KAREN: Do they all wear watches thicker than their wrists?

SAM: The thicker, the richer.

KAREN: Is it because of all the diamonds inside?

SAM: No they're on the soles of their Ferragamos. Karen, I bet I could get him to designate his annual donation to fund a development director position.

ACT ONE; SCENE TWO

KAREN: Brilliant, Sam, that's brilliant. You could raise the rest in a flash.

SAM: The thing is, I don't know whether it's ethical to steer his donation in a particular direction without input from the board.

KAREN: Why not?

SAM: Because it benefits me.

KAREN: It benefits the Matrix Foundation because it lets you do your job. If the board has some different idea about how Matrix can use his money, they can suggest it.

SAM: Maybe I should talk to a few of the board.

KAREN: Whatever, but you don't need to and if they object, quit.

SAM: Not now with a baby coming.

KAREN: Bullshit. We still have 250K left from the inheritance. We could live off that until you found some another gig. I bet there are a dozen foundations out there who would kill to have you as their director.

SAM: And be full-time parents in the meantime--especially if they're twins.

KAREN: I'd be bored in a week.

SAM: Joking.

KAREN: Sam, I want to go back to work as soon as I can.

SAM: Fine with me, I'll stay at home.

[He reaches for her. She responds.]

KAREN: You look so happy.

SAM: Happy as I've ever been.

BLACK OUT

ACT ONE; SCENE THREE
ZEKE'S OUT-DOOR DINING DECK

Sam texts at a table that has been cleared of everything but coffee cups, a bottle of cognac and glasses. Eric enters and slides into the seat across from Sam.

ERIC: You were fucking brilliant. They loved you, guy, loved you. I can't believe Ravi Nir tried to blow me off with 10K. I told him he needed to double it and make it an annual commitment.

SAM: What did he say?

ERIC: Squirmed. Ravi always squirms. "Eric my boy, I have need to think about it, eh?"

SAM: I'd take 10K in a nanosecond.

ERIC: I said to him, "Ravi, you drop 100K every time your plane hits the tarmac in Vegas. I want 20K a year or I pay your favorite holy man a million dollars to reincarnate you as a cockroach!"

[Eric pulls the check out of his pocket and flips it over to Sam.]

ERIC: First installment.

SAM: You're amazing Eric, we got to get you on our board.

ERIC: Ravi's got a big heart. Liam's good for ten, Newsom for five. Bob and Luke are over-invested but they are in on a block-buster IPO next year and then they're good for big money.

SAM: Thank you so much, Eric.

ERIC: I'm just the closer; you hooked them.

SAM: That was gutsy--to challenge Ravi like that. I'm always unsure when to push harder.

ACT ONE; SCENE THREE

ERIC: Ravi has more money than God. His old man runs Microsoft in Russia. Ravi says he works out with Putin.

SAM: That's scary.

ERIC: Now you know why Apple can forget Russia.

SAM: Would I have heard of Bob and Luke's IPO?

ERIC: It's confidential. They're hip-pocket investors.

SAM: How do you mean?

ERIC: Before a company goes public, SEC limits the number of investors. The way this is commonly gotten around is that the original investors take on hip-pocket investors by selling them a portion of their shares. Generally it is treated with a wink and a nod but there is always a potential that if the SEC gets wind of a particular transaction the secondary investors could be stripped of their shares.

SAM: Got it. Sorry, didn't mean to pry.

ERIC: Sam, ask me anything you want about my world. You're welcome to it.

SAM: Eric it's amazing, I feel Matrix is reaching a new level as a foundation, thanks to you.

ERIC: Awesome!

SAM: It's a day of good news. I just heard from Karen. She's definitely pregnant.

ERIC: Congratulations!
  [Toasting]
To your lovely wife and the next generation.

SAM *[Toasting]:* To Eric Deveraux who in a short time has done so much for Matrix. Felicidades!

ERIC: Felicidades!
  [Eric offers Sam a cigar from a leather case.]

ERIC: A smoke.

SAM: Thanks

[Looking at the band]

These are Cubans?

ERIC: Monte Cristo twos.

SAM: Wow.

They both light up....And enjoy...

ERIC: They're from Ravi. He's placed puts on the reopening of trade between U.S. and Cuba. Every time he goes to Havana he comes back with a box.

SAM: How does he get through customs?

ERIC: Private jet with State Department clearance. No problem.

SAM: I've heard about Cristos but I never smoked one. They really are different.

ERIC: You can't beat that smooth, rich cedary flavor.

SAM: Yeah.

ERIC: Sam, can I ask you a question?

SAM: Of course.

ERIC: If there is one thing you could have for Matrix what would it be?

SAM: Actually, Eric, I wanted to reach out to you about something.

ERIC: Go for it.

SAM: When I came on as executive director, Matrix was essentially a conduit for its board members' charities. As I told you I got them to focus on environmental justice. Subsequently we've doubled our donations but also the number of grants. As a result I spend ninety percent of my time fund raising and maybe ten percent of my time mentoring the programs we fund.

ERIC: And that's what you love?

SAM: You got it. Otherwise I'm just another foundation bureaucrat.

ACT ONE; SCENE THREE

ERIC: It's like reading prospectuses. I have to prop my eyes open with toothpicks. What I love is going into the field and checking out start-ups ---trying to pick the one in a thousand that's going to put hair on my chest.

SAM: What I'd like to do is to hire a full-time fund raiser that would free me to spend more time developing programs that would have a national scope.

ERIC: Cut to the chase, guy. What do you want me to do to get you one?

SAM: What I wanted you to consider is turning your annual donation, not the one you just gave, but the next two years as part of a challenge grant to raise money to pay the salary of a fund raiser/ development director.

ERIC: How much?

SAM: A decent fund raiser with benefits, about 100K. If you would earmark your donation and maybe get Ravi to earmark his to fund the position that gives me 80K with which to go to one of the major, endowed foundations for a grant to cover the rest--

ERIC: I'm in.

SAM: You sure?

ERIC: Absolutely. But let me ask you a question. With a good fund raiser, you develop more programs, and in a few years you'll be right where you are now. Am I right?

SAM: Well, hopefully we'll also collect more generous donors but yeah, in my world poverty is a by-product of success. The only foundations that don't have to spend a humongous time raising money have an endowment that covers their grants.

ERIC: O.K. Let's put together an endowment.

SAM: It would take a ridiculous amount of money.

BIG MONEY

ERIC: How much would you need? We're just talking.

SAM: Well, last year we gave out two point seven million in grants with an operating budget of about 300K.

ERIC: To be conservative we'll guess-timate a seven percent return on capital...you'd need about a forty million endowment to cover it all.

SAM: We're so, so far away from that.

ERIC: Sam, give me your vision of Matrix if we could figure out how to raise an endowment for you.

SAM: I would like to see Matrix move away from being primarily a granting foundation to one that also initiates and funds its own programs.

ERIC: Tell me about the first program you would fund with a new endowment?

SAM: I want to start a school to train organizers for the environmental justice movement. Time and time again, you see projects imploding because of inexperience and lack of training in basic organizing tactics. I see it being somewhere between an academic fellowship program and community hands-on training where student organizers would intern with on-going successful programs and organizers.

ERIC: What else?

SAM: Bad News is a collective of internet journalists who I have been in discussions with about organizing an environmental justice news syndicate. I have been trying to get them funding for three years.-- Medical students in Louisiana need funding to set-up community and work based environmental watch groups in five towns on cancer alley and hire an organizer to start programs like their's at other medical schools.

ERIC: Got it. Ten years down the road, what is your vision for yourself and Matrix. Where would you like to be?

ACT ONE; SCENE THREE

SAM: Matrix, right now does a tremendous amount of good on the local level. We've helped hundreds of environmental justice campaigns accomplish their goals but it's a little like whack-a mole, as soon as you slam one another pops up. My dream is that Matrix brings environmental justice issues to the fore of the national political debate. Five years, ten years, whatever, I want to make environmental justice crucial enough that our political representatives would be elected because of their support for them not defeated because of it.

ERIC: Wow.

SAM: A bit of a pipe dream.

ERIC: In my world it all starts with pipe dreams.

SAM: Eric, I'm open to any ideas. If you know of anyone who might be receptive to donating that type of money I would absolutely love to meet them.

ERIC: I was looking at your web-site the other day and I couldn't figure out your board.

SAM: How do you mean?

ERIC: How do they make their money?

SAM: Mostly they inherited it. The core group founded Matrix as a way to organize their charitable giving to have the most effect.

ERIC: I assume the board is Matrix's main money source.

SAM: Eighty percent if you count their close friends and relatives.

ERIC: They're full-time philanthropists?

SAM: They all work even if it's volunteering. We have three teachers, a couple of arts administrators, an acupuncturist, two doctors who work at free clinics, a published author, three lawyers who work pro bono, and a professor/documentary film maker.

ERIC: What's their aggregate worth?

BIG MONEY

SAM: Everyone is pretty discreet about their financial resources.

ERIC: Afraid you'll go after them for a bigger bite?

SAM: Actually, I think they're embarrassed by their wealth.

ERIC: I don't get that. You'd think they'd feel lucky.

SAM: They do, but they also feel that whatever they give is not enough--which isn't true by the way.

ERIC: They're good people, I got that, but what do you think they're worth--all together?

SAM: I could be way off but the whole board from what they've said, counting all their assets, I'd guess around three hundred million.

ERIC: That's your endowment right there.

SAM: I don't understand.

ERIC: It's in front of your nose, guy. That's the resource you use to raise your endowment. Listen I got a meeting I'm late for but let's make a date...

[Checking his iPhone]

Shit, I'm out of town next three weeks...oh then I'm gone again... Here's an idea on the 23rd of next month I'm flying to Austin to kick some tires. Why don't you come with and we'll brainstorm on the way there and back.

SAM *[Checking his iPhone]:* I'm supposed to go to a fund raiser that night with Karen. I can beg off-

ERIC: Not a problem, we're taking my plane. It's only a three hour flight. I'll pick you up early AM and have you back in the city by 6-7 at the latest.

SAM: That'll work.

ERIC: Fantastic, guy, we're on.

SAM: I've never flown on a private plane.

ERIC: Get used to it guy--Ciao.

[As Eric leaves, Sam notices Eric's cigar case on the table.]

ACT ONE; SCENE THREE

SAM: Eric!... You forgot your cigars.
ERIC: Enjoy.
   [Eric exits stage right.]

BLACK OUT

BIG MONEY

ACT ONE; SCENE FOUR
LOFT--LATER

Karen talks on the phone. She wears a wind-breaker with MARINE MAMMAL RESCUE CENTER inscribed on its back. The makings for a knitting project are on the table beside her. Sam enters.

KAREN *[Hanging up]:* Got to go babe-- call me when you get results from the cultures.

[They kiss.]

ERIC: Something going on?

KAREN: A couple of harbor seals that were brought in have some weird skin rash. We're culturing it. You smell like cigar.

SAM: Eric had some Cubans.

KAREN: Lucky dog.

SAM: Want to try one? He gave me these.

[She takes one, smells it and hands it back.]

KAREN: In seven months and twenty-three days.

SAM: We'll save them.

KAREN: Fat chance. Look.

[She produces the sonogram]

There she is.

SAM: A girl, you didn't tell me that. Now we only have to think girl names. She could be Sam--antha

KAREN: Sounds like a pole dancer. A name should be a blank page.

SAM: Baby Michaels-Garcia until she's fifteen. She'll name herself at her quinceaniera.

KAREN: Hyphenated names are bullshit, Rachel Garcia is fine.

SAM: Rachel?

ACT ONE; SCENE FOUR

KAREN: If you like it. My favorite Aunt's name.

SAM: She's the one who took you around Paris dressed in drag.

KAREN: The Gertrude Stein tour.

SAM: Rachel Garcia...O.K. Not quite a blank page

   [He picks up the sonogram and studies it.]

Where is she?

KAREN: That little dot circled with a sharpie.

SAM: It looks like she's in the center of a cosmic cyclone... I didn't know they could tell the sex this early.

KAREN: They can't do the test for 3 weeks. But I know.

SAM: Let's not have a boy named Rachel--he'll kill us.

KAREN: It's a girl, I can sense it.

SAM: Are you going mystical on me?

KAREN: I do have a cosmic cyclone in my womb.

SAM: What else did the doctor have to say?

KAREN: I'm in good health, I have a fine pelvis, and come back in a month.

   [Sam pulls out a couple of ales, offering Karen one.]

KAREN: And one drink a week, which I had at lunch.

SAM: Could they tell if it is all right?

KAREN: She. They run tests the next visit.

SAM: For what specifically--the sex?

KAREN: If we want. Downs and everything that's more likely if the mother is over thirty-five.

SAM: She'll be fine...

KAREN: I'm not really worried, but you read all-

SAM: She or he or both will be fine.

KAREN: If I have two, I'm giving one to Polly.

SAM: No way. Tell her to make her own.

KAREN: Enough baby talk. What did Deveraux say about earmarking his contribution for a development director?

SAM: He'll do it, but what really seems to get him hot is helping us establish an endowment.

KAREN: Sam, that's great. Do you think he's planning on some super gift?

SAM: I'm flying with him to Austin to check-out a start-up he's interested in. He wants to talk about it then.

KAREN: I finally googled him. He's involved in a thousand different deals.

SAM: He raised thirty-five thousand at the lunch today and twenty of it is an annual pledge.

KAREN: Wow! From whom?

SAM: Three friends of his--I haven't had a chance to check them out but the annual pledge is from Ravi Nir. Eric says his father runs Microsoft in Russia.

KAREN: Does he work for Microsoft too?

SAM: He's a commodities trader. Eric says he's making a big bet on whether Obama will lift the Cuba trade embargo.

KAREN: How do you do that?

SAM: Buy or short grain futures I suppose.

KAREN: Which side is he taking?

SAM: Probably both.

KAREN: Sounds evil.

SAM: What do you mean?

KAREN: The trade embargo hurts so many people-- A whole country. I don't think you should make money off it.

SAM: Or lose it.

KAREN: How do you see it?

SAM: It's another crafty way finance capitalists make their billions.

KAREN: Seriously.

SAM: I don't see commodity speculation, as any more evil than

ACT ONE; SCENE FOUR

any other type of speculation--maybe less so. You aren't shorting a stock so that a company goes bankrupt and people are thrown out of work. You aren't speculating on liar loans that throw families out of their homes. You aren't investing in land mines or prisons--

KAREN: They all suck.

SAM: Down with capitalism but first make your donation.

KAREN: That's cynical.

SAM: It's reality. Capitalism rules so you have to find ways to deal with it or else you go crazy or become a terrorist which is sort of the same thing.

KAREN: Do you ever wish we were back fighting the whalers?

SAM: Hard with a bad leg and a baby, but yeah, no bullshit, just good guys, bad guys and you.

KAREN: Sometimes I see you looking at the photo of us together on the bridge. Is that when you are missing it?

[Sam picks up the photo and looks at it.]

SAM: I don't know, It's a great photo.

KAREN: Marlie took it right after we moved our stuff into the same cabin.

SAM: It's sort of a marriage photo.

KAREN: Better than...

[Checking her i-pad]

When did you say you're going to Austin?

SAM: Twenty-third of next month.

KAREN: We have tickets to the Burning Spear concert--it's a fund raiser for The Center.

SAM: I'll be back by six or seven. Eric is taking his plane.

KAREN: Living large.

SAM: Somebody has to do it.

KAREN: Capitalist dog.

[She swats at him, playful. He takes her hand. Picking up the beginnings of a knitting project on the counter.]

SAM: What are you making?

KAREN: Rachel's blanket. Polly gave me a bag of wool from her sheep.

SAM: I didn't know you knew how to knit.

KAREN: I don't. I'm trying to get into this motherhood thing.

SAM: Love you.

[They kiss.]

BLACK OUT

ACT ONE; SCENE 5
AUSTIN; PRIVATE AIRPORT LOUNGE - A MONTH LATER

P.A. SPEAKER: Mr. Munson your plane is fueled and waiting on the tarmac.

[Sam and Eric, wearing identical suede jackets, sit at a cocktail table, Eric nursing a Red Bull, Sam, a beer.]

ERIC: Guy, don't keep me in suspense. What did you think of T/Q Dynamics?

SAM: You just shot way past my level of incompetence.

ERIC: Your take. Are they the next big launch off the medical device platform or bullshit?

SAM: Their kinetic models are amazing...Karen would have loved to see them.

ERIC: What about Joe and Wayne?

SAM: Nice guys. Good energy. Are you going to invest?

ERIC: Haven't decided. If they came to Matrix with an idea or what do you call it--organizing project, would you fund it?

SAM: If I was excited about the idea, they had a good plan, and if Matrix had the money, I'd certainly take a serious look. But I agree leadership is key--an iffy plan can succeed with good leadership but not the other way around.

ERIC: It's who's taking it to the show. Even after your quant's run metrics that would do a colostomy proud, it's the leadership. I've been close to so many start-ups that look like Microsoft then explode quicker than a roadside bomb. When you drill down, the cause is almost always leadership fuck-up.

SAM: Ultimately there's no way to know for sure.

ERIC: I've given some serious thought to Feng Shui---a joke--though I've heard rumors that Kleiner Perkins has a Feng

Shui priest on call. What I do is after all the reports say it's a sure thing--another Apple, blah, blah blah. I get right in the their faces. I mean eye-to-eye with the principals and if I can see them crossing the finish line---They give me that confidence. I buy in.

SAM: How often are you right?

ERIC: I've easily read over ten thousand business plans. To date I've invested in eighty-six start-ups out of which five have produced an eight figure pay-out. Of the others some did modestly well, some did modestly not so well.

SAM: What was your biggest?

ERIC: Google. I got in on one of the later rounds but I still made almost nine figures.

SAM: Wow!

ERIC: How about you, what goes into your calculus?

SAM: Ultimately, when all the reviews are in and everything looks good, it's a subjective call 80-90 percent based on the leadership....For instance with the Eden Gardens, the key was Butch Taylor. He was featured in the article you read. Five minutes into a meeting with him I was ready to throw a grant at him for anything he wanted to do. He had a magnetism and energy and this open sincerity that drew you in--- what I'd call a born organizer.

ERIC: How did Joe and Wayne rank against Taylor?

SAM: That's a pretty high bar-

ERIC: When it's my money, that's where the bar sits. Thanks, guy, I agree. Now let's talk about an endowment fund for Matrix.

SAM: I've already opened a discussion with key board members and they're stoked. What I was thinking is a major donor campaign that would, with your help, reach out to the pro-

ACT ONE; SCENE 5

gressive community in The Gulch where, until you came into our lives, we had almost zero contacts. We were thinking an Environmental Justice Awards Dinner--With a celebrity MC. There is a good chance we could get Matt Damon.

ERIC: Award dinners are good but they aren't going to get Matrix an endowment.

SAM: But--

ERIC: Let me tell you a little bit about this company I've been nurturing for the last nine years because it could be key to getting this together.

SAM: Awesome, we're open to any ideas, especially from you..

ERIC: Xerxes Technology is the name of the company.

SAM: What do they do?

ERIC: They're a clean-tech company. I got my feet wet when it was nothing more than two guys and an idea. The two guys being Chuck Bonham and Jon Chen from Cal Tech, working evenings and weekends in a storage locker. Brilliant guys, that was clear right from the get-go but no business experience at all so I came on board as CEO to help raise capital and get the business side of their operation in order. It took most of my energy for the next couple of years and five private offerings until they had sufficient capital and I felt they were secure enough for me to step down. It took another four years and two more offerings to bring them to where they are now, which is they hold a patent on a bleeding edge system of photo-voltaic cells that can be built into the roof and hood of an electric car that will increase its average range four hundred percent.

SAM: Amazing.

ERIC: Last month Solar Systems offered to buy them out at a one-to-one peg.

SAM: What's a one-to-one peg?

ERIC: Solar Systems will give Xerxes shareholders one share of their stock, which is trading in the low thirties, for one share of Xerxes stock. I hold or have options on two point five million shares that I paid, on average, three dollars a share.

SAM: Wow, you'll make what?

ERIC: Seventy--eighty million, depending where the price of solar systems shares are at closing.

SAM: It's unreal.

ERIC: It's becoming very real. Xerxes and Solar Systems have completed three rounds of meetings. The basic parameters are essentially agreed upon.

SAM: Congratulations. What great news.

ERIC: For both of us. I've had my tax lawyers working out how we can transfer thirty million worth of Solar Systems shares I get from the Xerxes sale to Matrix.

SAM: Are you fucking serious!

ERIC: Sam, that's why I'm telling you about the deal. My first thought was to do it as a straight donation but the lawyers say there is no way I can do that without screwing myself on the taxes.

SAM: Wouldn't it be a tax deductible charitable donation?

ERIC: The problem is I could potentially be liable for capital gains taxes or even gift taxes but my lawyers have come up with an elegant solution. They propose we make Matrix co-investors by selling you a million and a half shares of my Xerxes holdings, which, when, converted into Solar Systems shares, will be worth between thirty and forty million.

SAM: Eric, I really appreciate this, but I don't see how your lawyer's plan will work if I understand it correctly. Matrix runs on a five percent deficit so there is no money to buy the shares.

ACT ONE; SCENE 5

ERIC: My bad. I'm not being clear. Matrix Foundation would not be a direct purchaser/investor. What you need to do, you and your board members, is set up a private investment group. Call it the Matrix Group or the Garcia group, whatever, and use it as a vehicle to buy shares of Xerxes from me at five dollars per share, which gives me a forty percent profit which should satisfy the IRS and then when the deal is finalized sell the shares and donate the proceeds to Matrix.

SAM: Got it, got it...I can see that working--theoretically

ERIC: You would be investing through me, as a hip pocket investor in the over-all deal.

SAM: It's a great opportunity--obviously- but it won't be easy. The Matrix community has a pretty negative attitude toward finance in general, and financial speculation is pretty much off the charts.

ERIC: I thought that people passionate about the environment would feel good about investing in a technology that increases the range of the electric cars.

SAM: And it's a car that everyone on our board would stand in line to buy. The question they'll raise is whether an environmental justice foundation that is committed to fighting social inequalities should be profiting from financial speculation which contributes to those inequalities.

ERIC: Would the Matrix board accept a grant from George Soros foundation or the Gates foundation?

SAM: Yes and we have. I guess when grants come from a foundation it is removed from its original source.

ERIC: Removed? How about laundered? Didn't Soros make his money cornering currency markets. As I recall he bankrupted a country or two?

SAM: I hear what you're saying.

ERIC: And all you're asking of them is to make a lot of money for the Matrix Foundation which they support and believe in by investing in a socially responsible, clean-tech product at virtually no risk.

SAM: Eric you don't have an argument with me. I'm all for it, it's a fantastic opportunity for Matrix. I can see a few getting involved.

ERIC: For how much?

SAM: I don't know...Maybe 400K.

ERIC: Shit, that's not going to do much.

SAM: We'll make four million---it's fucking fantastic.

ERIC: It isn't an endowment fund.

SAM: It's the beginning of one.

ERIC: No. Thirty million is an endowment fund; four gets pissed away.

SAM: Maybe there's another way to structure the transfer?

ERIC: No, I had two different tax attorneys look at it. What we'll do is sweeten the pot. We'll give Matrix donors an opportunity to purchase additional shares of Xerxes for themselves on a two for one basis.

SAM: Come again?

ERIC: Let's say a Matrix donor purchases a hundred thousand shares for Matrix. In consideration, we then give them the right to purchase what? Fifty thousand shares for themselves.

SAM: That's really generous of you. The problem I see is these folks are not super interested in accumulating more wealth. They are already uncomfortable with what they have.

ERIC: Sam, everyone wants more money. It's our DNA. You just have to give them the confidence that it is the right thing to do.

ACT ONE; SCENE 5

SAM: This is a fantastic opportunity and I'm going for it. All they can do is say no.

ERIC: Trust me they won't.

END OF ACT ONE

BIG MONEY

ACT TWO; SCENE ONE
LOFT

Sam enters. Karen, asleep on the couch, wakes as Sam sits down beside her. They kiss.

KAREN: Hi.

SAM: Hi, you all right?

KAREN: Just napping. We had three seals ready to be released so I pitched in.

SAM: You shouldn't be doing that now, it's dangerous.

KAREN: I was careful to stay out of the way of their flippers. Betty, my favorite, didn't want to go. She kept heading back up the beach and we kept blocking her way with the boards. It took over an hour, before she gave up. Right before she swam away, she turned and looked at me with those big sad seal eyes, as if to say "you traitor". I cried...

[Sam comforts her; Karen sucks it in.]

KAREN: Where'd you get the slick jacket?

SAM: A present from the company me and Eric visited. They gave each of us one.

KAREN: Nice. It went well?

SAM: I don't know how to describe it except that if it works it will transform Matrix. Totally.

KAREN: Yeah? Tell me.

SAM: How does a thirty million dollar endowment fund for Matrix strike you?

KAREN: Omigod, is it for real?

SAM: As far as I can tell.

KAREN: Come on tell me more!

SAM: We better book or we'll be late for the concert.

KAREN: Let's blow it off. I want to hear about this.

ACT TWO; SCENE ONE

SAM: You sure.

KAREN: Yeah. Now tell me about it.

SAM: It's pretty complicated but Xerxes Technology, a start-up Eric invested in a number of years ago – actually he was their CEO for awhile – is being bought by Solar Systems.

KAREN: Who they?

SAM: It's the biggest clean-tech company in the world.

KAREN: Oh, is that all--and Xerxes?

SAM: It's a start-up founded by a couple of Cal Tech guys that have developed a proprietary technology for solar panels that can be attached to the roof of an electric car that will increase its range four-fold.

KAREN: Amazing.

SAM: Eric says he'll make seventy to eighty million off the sale; thirty million of which he wants to give to Matrix to set up an endowment fund.

KAREN: Omigod, Sam.

SAM: Eric's already talked to his tax attorney on how to structure the gift, which involves us buying one point five million shares of Xerxes from Eric for five dollars a share which would then be converted to an equal number of shares of Solar System which trades in the low thirties netting us roughly thirty million dollars.

KAREN: But how can Matrix buy millions of dollars worth of stock?

SAM: What I have to do is convince our board and major donors to set up an investment group through which they can buy the shares from Eric and when the deal closes, sell their shares of Solar Systems and donate their profits to Matrix.

KAREN: What happens if it doesn't close?

SAM: It's already being finalized. What I'm worried about is convincing the board to get behind it.

KAREN: It's everything you wanted.

SAM: Yeah. Potentially Matrix will have an endowment fund with an annual income of almost three million.

KAREN: Wow Sam. Wow! It takes your breath away.

SAM: When Eric told me I thought I was going to lose it.

KAREN: I'm so happy, Sam, you've worked so hard ...I am losing it...

[They hug.]

KAREN: I hope people will feel comfortable about doing it. They really don't know Eric--

SAM: He gave Matrix sixty-thousand dollars, and raised another 35K from his friends, what more do they need to know? What I'll propose to the board and major donors is that they use their annual donation to Matrix to purchase shares of Xerxes. In that way it won't be such a big bite.

KAREN: What are you going to do about grants that are coming due?

SAM: I think we have enough in reserve to cover them and by the time the next disbursements are due the deal will be way closed.

KAREN: Is there a time-line for raising the money?

SAM: We have sixty days to set up a limited partnership, hire a transaction attorney to do the due diligence and set up the deal with Eric's company, hire an accountant, hire a tax attorney to make sure everything complies with various rules and regulations, and ten other things I wrote down. My brain is on overload with the details Eric shot at me.

[Sam cracks open a beer and takes a long drink.]

KAREN: Maybe it would be helpful to give my brother a call. His firm has a lot of clients from the I/T world. He might have some advice about a lawyer and other stuff

ACT TWO; SCENE ONE

SAM: This isn't rocket science, but that's an idea, if I have a question I can't get answered. The key problem at the moment is convincing the board to put on their Nikes and raise and donate some serious money.

KAREN: How do you think they'll react?

SAM: In their usual snail-like fashion.

KAREN: Are any of them around the I/T world?

SAM: Socially, maybe, but we don't have anybody on our board really knowledgeable. Eric offered what he called a sweetener. He will allocate another bunch of his Xerxes shares to board members to buy as a private investment that we'll peg to how many shares they buy for Matrix.

KAREN: Do you think people will want to do it?

SAM: We'll see. From a business standpoint it is a fantastic deal.

KAREN: It's so exciting Sam.

SAM: Karen, I was thinking that we should put some of the savings in the deal.

KAREN: Really? How much are you thinking?

SAM: Well, there's 250K in the bank.

KAREN: Sam, what if something happens?

SAM: Like what? We own the loft outright. Our jobs are secure.

KAREN: I don't know--what if the baby has problems?

SAM: She won't and besides we have good medical insurance.

KAREN: I don't know--I guess, it's something I never even thought about.

SAM: Karen, I don't want to do it if you aren't into it. It's your inheritance not mine.

KAREN: It's both our money Sam...

SAM: You say that but still-

KAREN: It seems if we are having children we should keep some savings.

BIG MONEY

SAM: What if we put in 150K? We'd end up with close to a million dollars. If we gave half the profit to the Matrix Endowment fund, we'd still have enough to buy some land along the coast.

KAREN: That would be so cool.

SAM: So we'll keep a 100K in reserve for an emergency?

KAREN: Let's do it.

SAM: You sure? I don't want to do this if-

KAREN: No, let's do it. I just hope this doesn't change us. I grew up around rich people and they weren't a very happy bunch.

SAM: I grew up around people who were always worried about not having enough money and they weren't very happy either--I don't think having or not having money is the issue--it's how you deal with it.

KAREN: No you're right--but let's be careful. O.K?

SAM: O.K... You know what?

KAREN: What.

SAM: I love you.

[A kiss/embrace]

KAREN: Now for more immediate matters, what do you want on your pizza?

SAM: The usual.

[They reach for their phones. Their calls overlap.]

KAREN: Hi Tony, this is Karen...we're doing fine and you...Right, the usual...you got it. Thanks a bunch...Ciao.

SAM: Hey Carl, Sam. Listen we need to get together soonest. I have just been presented with a fantastic opportunity for Matrix. If you pick this up maybe we could even get together later tonight or tomorrow morning. I'll be in by seven.

KAREN: Sam, she kicked.

[Karen puts his hand on her stomach.]

ACT TWO; SCENE ONE

KAREN: She's moving. Can you--

SAM: No. What did it feel like?

KAREN: Gentle- like a nudge or like a shifting...there.

SAM: Yeah, yeah I feel her. Amazing...

BLACK OUT

BIG MONEY

ACT TWO; SCENE TWO
SAM'S OFFICE - TWO MONTHS LATER

Eric and Sam, Red Bulls beside them, sit across from one another signing the last item from four stacks of documents. Eric signs the last document and passes it to Sam.

SAM: I've never signed so many documents.
ERIC: What makes my world go round.
　[Separating the piles]
　Yours, mine, and we're done!
SAM: Right on!
　[A fist-bump].
SAM: Going into this I had my doubts about our board but I was totally wrong. They really got it.
ERIC: It was a real lesson to me how you reached out with such patience and understanding not to mention perseverance.
SAM: I thought there would be more resistance.
ERIC: You gave them confidence that you could turn Matrix into a major force for environmental justice. "An awesome responsibility" That was brilliant. You put it right on them.
SAM: Because it's true. But your generosity set the tone for everyone.
ERIC: I'm honored to have played a role, speaking of which I better get these to my lawyers so we can start moving things along.
SAM: Do we have a specific date yet when the shares will be exchanged?
ERIC: Not a date certain but in the next several weeks. We have to get the approval of the overall deal by SEABEC but it's a formality.
SAM: What's SEABEC?

ACT TWO; SCENE TWO

ERIC: Sorry. The Southeast Asia Board of Economic Competition.

SAM: When does that happen?

ERIC: They meet the end of the quarter--so next month.

SAM: The shares are distributed then?

ERIC: There's always some clean-up work after... I'd say four to six weeks after.

SAM: I thought it would be sooner. Matrix makes its fiscal year disbursements to its grantees July 1st, so we're cutting it pretty close.

ERIC: No worries. The deal should close by June at the latest.

SAM: The groups we fund are pretty bare bones so it would create a big mess if we're late.

ERIC: You'll definitely have your Solar stocks by then. If you can't cash them immediately you always have the option of borrowing against them.

SAM: Why wouldn't we be able to cash them in? I thought--

ERIC: Hopefully you can, but often in a deal this size there's a ninety day hold so as not to disrupt the market.

SAM: You think it's likely?

ERIC: Fifty-fifty. This is a big deal and they go by the rules... Listen, if there's any problem in meeting your deadlines. I'll guarantee whatever you're short.

SAM: I don't know exactly what our reserve is but we could run short by as much as 200K.

ERIC: Not a problem. I'll either raise it or cover it.

SAM: Thank you Eric, that's perfect. I guess we're good to go.

ERIC: You got it...

[Eric pulls out his cigar case, offering one to Sam.]

ERIC: Can we smoke these in here?

SAM: Everyone's gone for the day so let's just do it.

ERIC: Right on.

[The men prepare their cigars and light up.].

ERIC: Sam, you know your people are going to be good deal richer when this closes.

SAM: Yeah, we'll be moving up to the big leagues--or at least triple A--I've already talked to a few people about forming an exploratory committee for the organizers' school.

ERIC: Awesome. How much are you and Karen going to clear?

SAM: Solar Systems closed today at 32?

ERIC: And I think they had a bump after hours.

SAM: Let's say 32. We paid $5 a share for 30,000 shares so...

ERIC: Over 800K--not bad. What are you going to do with it?

SAM: Half goes to Matrix.

ERIC: And the rest?

SAM: We've been talking about getting some land up the coast.

ERIC: Land is pretty expensive up there. Maybe we should look around for another investment.

SAM: I'd certainly be open to it. I'd have to run it by Karen.

ERIC: There are a couple of platforms that are beginning to cook. We'll find something good.

SAM: Let me know.

ERIC: Count on it.

SAM: You know I was pretty sure I could convince people to use their annual donation to buy Xerxes stock for Matrix but I was totally surprised how much of a personal investment people made.

ERIC: Why wouldn't they? We're offering them an opportunity of a lifetime.

SAM: They're always talking about the problems managing their money. I didn't think they'd be that interested in accumulating more.

ACT TWO; SCENE TWO

ERIC: Don't get me wrong Sam, your board--they're good people-- but when people complain about having problems with money, it means one thing--they want more of it.

SAM: Not necessarily.

ERIC: Did any of them offer to donate the profit from their personal share to Matrix?

SAM: Why should they?

ERIC: Because having too much money is such a problem.

SAM: ...I hear what you're saying...

[Eric shovels his documents into a file case.]

SAM: Are you in town for a while?

ERIC: Hong Kong next week...Geneva two weeks later. I'll be running like crazy.

SAM: Karen and I wanted to get you over for dinner.

ERIC: I'd love that. I've never seen your loft. You know I've been thinking about getting a place in the city.

SAM: Call me when you figure out when you'll be in town.

ERIC: Will do. And let's cut out time to sit down and talk some other projects.

SAM: I'd like that... Safe journeys.

[A manly embrace.]

BLACK OUT

BIG MONEY

ACT TWO; SCENE THREE
THE LOFT - MONTHS LATER

Eric and Karen, visibly pregnant, relax in the sitting area. Sam puts together coffee and desert in the kitchen area.

ERIC: Sam's risotto was to die for.

KAREN: In a past life I'm sure he was an Italian chef.

ERIC: Sam tells me you're a marine biologist?

KAREN: I work at the Marine Mammal Rescue Center.

ERIC: You do research?

KAREN: I started out in the lab. Now, mostly I coordinate the educational and outreach programs.

ERIC: Do you like it?

KAREN: I love it but this is so awesome what you and Sam are doing.

ERIC: Putting this deal together for Matrix is the most exciting thing I've done in years. I told Sam he'd given me a mission.

KAREN: Sam is so charged. Every day he finds another project he wants to fund. It's like Christmas.

ERIC: He's going to do great things.

KAREN: I'm so proud of him...

ERIC: Sam told me your parents were Hollywood writers.

KAREN: For TV.

ERIC; What shows?

KAREN: They worked for a lot of the sitcoms in the Seventies and Eighties--All in the Family, Maude, The Jeffersons were the main ones.

ERIC: I loved those shows. They still writing?

KAREN: They're both dead-- for some time.

ERIC: They must have been young when they passed?

KAREN: Early fifties.

ACT TWO; SCENE THREE

ERIC: That's why I say you should live life to the fullest because you never know.

KAREN: Actually they had a pretty good idea.

ERIC: Cancer?

KAREN: Cirrhosis.

ERIC: That must of been hard for you.

KAREN: It affected my brother more than me. Are your parents still alive?

ERIC: Mom is. She's in an assisted living center back in Boston. Never misses a bingo game-- Hey Sam, you need any help?

SAM: Chill, I'm about done.

ERIC: You guys planning to have more than one child?

KAREN: Maybe. Do you want children?

ERIC: To be honest, no. I was a latchkey kid. I wouldn't know how to raise them.

KAREN: Any questions

[Indicating a stack on a table.]

There are books and books and books to answer them.

ERIC: I'd like a dog. That I could handle. A friend who volunteers at a shelter said she'd find me one.

KAREN: Any particular breed?

ERIC: I'll take any mutt as long as he'll run with me.

[Sam joins them with a tray of fruit, cheese and an elegant bottle of calvados. Eric checks the label.]

ERIC: Wow, this is some fine calvados.

SAM: Smells like an old apple orchard.

ERIC: I'll let you in on a secret. Terry's Liquors in Mountain View runs a special on this for two ninety-nine.

SAM: The best price in the city is three fifty.

KAREN: Isn't that incredibly cheap?

SAM: Three hundred and fifty dollars.

KAREN: Oh, not so cheap.

[On Eric's initiative they clink glasses.]

SAM: To the deal!

ERIC: To Matrix!

[Eric checks his watch, ready to leave.]

SAM: When do you think you'll get an official update on the buy-out?

ERIC: I'm sorry, I know I've been out of touch. Actually this afternoon we had a video conference with the team we have in place in Singapore. The long and short of it is that SEABEC is ready to sign off on the buy-out.

SAM: Fantastic. I checked with our bank. As long as we have the Solar Systems stock by the end of the month they'll lend us 250K on it to meet our grant obligations.

ERIC: We'd have to have the transfer done next week if you are really planning on using your Solar stock as collateral. In any case if we can't get it done by then, I have your grants covered. No worries.

SAM: What I'm hearing is that it is unlikely we'll have the shares in time?

ERIC: We have approval but they wanted some minor changes to do with liabilities in event of patent infringement suits. So the dance is both sides and their lawyers have to revise, review and sign off before the buy-out is officially approved.

KAREN: How long will that take?

ERIC: A few weeks at the outside. I know everything seems slow but given the context it is moving surprisingly fast.

KAREN: I don't understand what you mean about the context?

ERIC: The transfer of close to a billion dollars of which we're a small piece. The major players in the deal have Gulfstreams full of $2500 per hour lawyers, who need to look like they earn it. Big money moves slowly.

ACT TWO; SCENE THREE

SAM: So we need to make the arrangements to cover our grants.

ERIC: We'll get a loan from a boutique bank I use. I already talked to George Kelly who runs it about the possibility that we might need a short term loan. He said he'd be happy to arrange a line of credit at prime plus one for the Matrix Group.

SAM: I thought you were going cover the grant money?

ERIC: I was planning to take a loan out to cover your grants but the lawyers said there was a potential conflict of interest. Luckily, Kelly agreed to write a loan directly to you guys.

SAM: Oh...

KAREN: What is the conflict?

ERIC: They cited two different SEC regulations and an IRS provision that seem to prohibit it but I haven't examined it in detail.

SAM: Joe Starobin who's one of our major donors, is a corporate lawyer. Maybe he could give us a second opinion.

ERIC: Sure and then we're obliged to hire a third lawyer to weigh the two opinions and give his own opinion about which of the two other opinions are right and by then we've paid the lawyers more than double what we would pay in interest.

KAREN: Wouldn't Joe do it pro-bono?

ERIC: It's your call but from my perspective the interest I'd pay on a ninety day loan for Matrix to cover the grants is about half what I would pay my lawyer if we go a couple of rounds on the conflict question.

SAM: That makes sense.

[Eric passes a business card to Sam.]

ERIC: The bank's Bonita Savings. Give Kelly a call Monday morning. He's good people, you'll like him.

SAM: Are there any other steps before we actually have the shares?

ERIC: We need to do a series of regulatory filings. Next up is NAFTA's competition commission. But it's all pro-forma.

KAREN: Why do you say it's pro-forma?

ERIC: Because I've been through it a dozen times before. You go before a hearing officer, he looks over the papers, and gives his approval.

KAREN: What if he or she doesn't approve it?

ERIC: It's referred to a hearing before the full commission. Look, it's going fine--not fast but chugging along. We've gotten EU approval, and preliminary approval from the SEC.

SAM: I didn't know we got EU approval.

ERIC: A few weeks back. Sorry, I must have forgotten to tell you. It's the same boring dance. We send them the papers, they send us the questions, we give the correct answers and a million or so later in legal and conveyance fees, they bless the buy-out and we're on our way.

KAREN: What about the SEC?

ERIC: No problem, the SEC isn't going to be the skunk at the wedding.

KAREN: Why wouldn't they?

ERIC: Because the hard truth is that Solar Systems is a Fortune 500 company and the deal has been given international approval by two of the major trade organizations. The SEC has no interest in gumming up the works. We're 97% the way there--we can't do any better than that.

SAM

[Cutting Karen off]

Gotcha.

KAREN

[getting up]

Guys excuse me but I had a killer day at the center and need to hit the sack. Eric so wonderful to get a chance to spend an evening with you.

[Eric gets up; Sam doesn't.]

ERIC: Thank you so much for sharing your evening with me. You know if you send me something about your center, I'd like to make a contribution.

KAREN: That would be great, I'll get a packet together for you.

[Karen's extended hand to Eric collapses into a awkward hug. Karen exits and Eric returns to his seat.]

SAM: Uno más?

ERIC *[placing his hand over glass]:* I'm driving.

SAM: How about a Red Bull?

ERIC: Does a bear shit in the woods?

[Sam retrieves a Red Bull from the refrigerator and pours himself another calvados.]

ERIC: Thanks, guy.

SAM: How long will it take to set up the loan?

ERIC: Forty-eight hours. You'll have to round up something for collateral.

SAM: I thought the loan was on the deal?

ERIC: Before the meltdown Kelly would have never asked for collateral but with all the new regulations the SEC has everybody looking over their shoulder. I'll tell you what, I'll offer an additional thirty thousand shares of Xerxes at six dollars a share to anyone who puts up the collateral.

SAM: We paid 600K cash for the loft.

ERIC: That would be perfect.

SAM: I'll have to run it by Karen.

ERIC: Must be some others in the Matrix group that could cover it. Karen seems a little nervous-

SAM: No, we should do it.

ERIC: What about the extra shares?

SAM: That's going to be a stretch.

ERIC: Sam, you're a stand-up guy. Matrix is lucky to have you.

SAM: I hope so.

ERIC: They are, believe me. The best thing for me about the Xerxes deal is getting to know you. You've opened my eyes on so many different levels. Thanks, guy...

[A moment of emotion subsumed in a fist bump. Eric drains his Red Bull.]

ERIC: Well, I better book. I'm off to Singapore tomorrow.

SAM: When are you back?

ERIC: I'll be in and out.

SAM: I guess we'd better make arrangements about the interest.

ERIC: Let me know when you have the loan nailed and I'll send you the first month's.

SAM: I thought...

ERIC: What?

SAM: Nevermind it's all right.

ERIC: What?

SAM: What should we do about the fees?

ERIC: When you get the damage send it my way.

SAM: I'm sorry for all the questions but this is all new to me and the Matrix Group members have been coming at me.

ERIC: Remind them that they have a buy-back clause--really. That'll cool them out. You're dealing with amateurs. They get nervous.

SAM: Yeah, I've been finding that out.

ERIC: Did you see where Solar Systems closed today?

SAM: Thirty-five and a half.

ERIC: So Matrix Groups' shares are worth?

SAM: Thirty-three million.`

ACT TWO; SCENE THREE

ERIC: Most analysts are saying Solar is going to hit forty-five by the end of the year.

SAM: It truly is an amazing deal.

ERIC: But you can't push it, and from where I'm sitting, given the current direction of Solar Systems stock, I don't mind the wait.

SAM: Neither do I.

ERIC: How much are your shares worth as of today?

SAM: Over a million but half goes to Matrix.

ERIC: You should be able to get a decent piece of land for that.

[Eric slides into his jacket.]

SAM: And hopefully enough at least to pull an RV onto it.

ERIC: Build a house, guy, you deserve it.

[Eric gets up and Sam walks him to the door.]

ERIC: Hey thanks again for dinner and thank Karen for me. You got yourself one fine lady.

SAM: She's a little nervous about all this. I think a lot of it is the baby.

ERIC: Listen, guy, if you want those extra shares, they're yours for three. If I have to pay gift taxes on them--so be it.

SAM: That's really generous. Can we talk later?

ERIC: Later it is. Give Kelly my best.

[They Embrace. Sam closes the door behind Eric. Lights up in bedroom area. Karen is in bed with her I-Pad. As Sam undresses.]

SAM: What are you reading?

KAREN: Crib ads. Are you worried?

SAM: About what?

KAREN: The delay.

SAM: Big money moves slowly.

KAREN: Didn't Eric say that?

BIG MONEY

SAM: Yeah, so what?

KAREN: Do you think he would have told you about the delay if you hadn't asked him?

SAM: Of course.

KAREN: He was practically putting on his coat when you did.

SAM: He was sitting across from me on the couch. Listen, Eric is involved in I don't know how many deals. He likes us and all but he's got a lot happening.

KAREN: It seems weird. You'd think if he knew there was a delay he would have gotten in touch with you before tonight.

SAM: We've been playing phone tag for most of last week. In any case he arranged for us to cover the grants that are due but we're going to have to put up something for collateral.

KAREN: Why?

SAM: Because bank loans require it. Eric is offering to sell thirty thousand Xerxes shares to the people who put it up.

KAREN: Sam, why did you cut me off?

SAM: When? I don't--

KAREN: When I was asking Eric about the SEC hearing--you jumped in and shut me up.

SAM: I'm sorry.

KAREN: You've never done that before.

SAM: I thought you were badgering him.

KAREN: I was trying get what he was saying.

SAM: I'm sorry Karen, I'm a little stressed ...Forgive me?

KAREN: It felt strange is all.

[A quick, make-up kiss.]

SAM: Do you know what Solar closed at today?

KAREN: Thirty-five and a half.

SAM: The analyst consensus calls it at forty-five by the end of the year, which means he's offering potentially a seven figure bonus to anybody who puts up the collateral.

ACT TWO; SCENE THREE

KAREN: It's like play money.

SAM: Would you be interested in putting up the collateral?

KAREN: We don't have--

SAM: We could take a loan out on the loft.

KAREN: We already put in over half of our savings.

SAM: Eric said if we wanted to do it he'd sell us the extra Xerxes shares at three dollars a share.

KAREN: Do we need to talk about this now. I have to get up early and-

SAM: Even at the current price the return for three months would be three quarters of a million dollars.

KAREN: I don't know Sam, why do we want all this money?

SAM: To get a place on the coast for one. Maybe buy a boat, set up an education account for the baby or--

KAREN: Buy three hundred dollar bottles of brandy.

SAM: I bought the calvados because Eric was coming over and I knew it was his favorite.

KAREN: I think it's obscene.

SAM: What was the two hundred dollar a bottle champagne you said your parents drank by the case?

KAREN: Obscene.

SAM: How can an excellent bottle of brandy or champagne in and of itself be obscene?

KAREN: Because millions of families in the world live on half that a year.

SAM: That's true and that is obscene but it has nothing to do with a bottle of excellent calvados that costs three hundred dollars which I bought to serve to Matrix's biggest donor...

KAREN: O.K. Buy a case of it.

[Karen turns away.]

SAM: So, what about taking a loan out on the loft?

KAREN: I don't want to put the loft up, Sam. I'm sorry but I don't.

SAM: Can I ask why?

KAREN: It's our home. We're going to have a baby in three months.

SAM: O.K.

KAREN: ... I don't understand why we're doing this in the first place.

SAM: To transform Matrix from a small foundation where my role is eighty percent overseeing other folks' charity projects, to an endowed foundation that has a national impact on the direction and strength of the movement for environmental justice.

KAREN: For Matrix it makes sense but why are we being sucked into it? I never even used to look at the business news, now the first thing I check is the Solar stock price. I even have it on my desk-top. It's money worship.

SAM: That's pretty simplistic. Not only is the technology we're investing in of incredible value to humankind but the capital we are making from "evil financial speculation" will directly benefit the fight for environmental justice which in my humble opinion makes whatever moral taint it leaves well worth it.

KAREN: But this is our home; it's where our child will be born.

SAM: People have mortgages on their homes--most people in fact--that is essentially what I'm asking you to do-- take out a ninety day mortgage. I don't see why it is such a big deal.

KAREN: It is a big deal, Sam, this whole thing has taken over our lives. It's not what I'm about. Not what we're about.

SAM: I'm about securing Matrix an endowment. It's about Matrix having a seat at the table in deciding the direction of environmental justice movement.

ACT TWO; SCENE THREE

KAREN: Is it that or is it about the million dollars we're going to make?

SAM: It's about both and I don't feel a need to apologize for it. Maybe because, unlike you, I've never had the comfort of money.

KAREN: Sam, I don't want to put up our home.

SAM: We aren't putting up our home we're taking a 90 day--

KAREN: I'm sorry.

SAM: Are you afraid of the risk because -

KAREN: I don't want to do it!

SAM: Fuck it then.

[Sam jumps out of bed and stalks downstage. The Bathroom door slams]

KAREN: Fuck you too.

[Lights fade on Karen, stifling angry tears.]

BIG MONEY

ACT TWO; SCENE FOUR
SAM'S OFFICE; MATRIX FOUNDATION

Eric sits beside Sam's desk talking on his phone and nursing a Red Bull. A warm smile greets Sam's entrance. He clicks off.

ERIC: Hi guy.
   [Sam sits in the chair across from Eric.]
SAM: Stay where you are. Sorry I'm late, I was meeting with Becky Clemens. I was hoping to get her to put up the collateral but she already used her house to bail Bradley Manning.
ERIC: Didn't you say Carl Boyce--
SAM: His money manager wouldn't let him. It's the same story right on down the board--either the money manager won't let them, their partner won't let them, their equity is tied up blah, blah, blah.
ERIC: You could always delay payments of the grants.
SAM: Not an option. My grantees would raise hell and rightfully so. I was wondering if you think we could approach Ravi Nir?
ERIC: He's in South Africa working with a start-up. You need it now.
SAM: I needed it yesterday---I got e-mails from three different projects asking where their money is.
ERIC: What does your board say?
SAM: Absolutely nothing which means it's my problem. Let the grantees dangle--'fuck 'em' in essence.
ERIC: Thought again about your loft?
SAM: There's nothing to think about. Karen won't do it.
ERIC: What if you talk to her again, explain the situation?
SAM: She's in LA visiting her brother. Maybe when she gets

ACT TWO; SCENE FOUR

back next week. But I can tell she's not going for it. She's got moral qualms or something.

ERIC: Too bad that would make it easy.

SAM: I don't know who to reach out to at this point...Any chance you could?

ERIC: I wish but I have no liquidity at the moment...

SAM: This is really fucked.

ERIC: You know, Sam, that as long as the signatures on the loan application match the ones on the deed the loan is yours.

SAM: ...I don't want to go there.

ERIC: We're talking a short term loan that's between you and the bank.

SAM: I just don't think I could do that.

ERIC: I know it's a tough one, guy...

SAM: I feel caught. Really caught. I couldn't believe that not one person on the board stepped up.

ERIC: Everyone's got their own priorities.

SAM: I mean I reached out to every one of them.

ERIC: Sam, you've gone the extra mile for those folks and then some...

SAM: You're saying as long as the signatures basically matched?

ERIC: Kelly's a friend.

SAM: He'll give me enough on the loft to cover the grants?

ERIC: Easily--more if you want it.

SAM: I don't know Eric, If Karen found out--

ERIC: Sam, let me share some personal history. A couple of times along the way when I needed to make things happen I made some moves that I'm not proud of--to this day. I told you I made nine figures on Google. What I didn't tell you was that I kited mortgages on four penthouses I owned in Miami Beach to raise the capital to buy those shares.

BIG MONEY

SAM: Wow.

ERIC: At the height I had three mortgages on the same property with three different brokers and don't think I didn't shit my pants thinking "what if". But, I'm glad I did it because I wouldn't be where I am today if I hadn't crossed some lines.

SAM: But this involves--

ERIC: Karen, I know, it's different for all of us... What can I say, it's just the nature of things--what you want, what you need to realize your dream never comes easy...Sometimes you just have to man up and take it on the chin. You're playing with the big boys now.

SAM: ...O.K. I'll go for it.

ERIC: Sam, for what it's worth I know what your going though. For me, I couldn't stop thinking how many years I'd spend in jail if somehow the one in a million happened and the deal unraveled, but I can tell you with confidence you made the right choice and so did I.

SAM: Thanks...

ERIC: What about shares for yourself?

SAM: We'll have this done at least by the end of next month?

ERIC: Sooner.

SAM: You were talking a while back about finding a few investments together.

ERIC: There's plenty of low hanging fruit out there.

SAM: I'll take them--the extra shares.

   [Eric's iphone rings.]

ERIC: Awesome. You should get to eat what you kill.

   [answers phone]

   Yeah I know. I'll be there ASAP.

   [Clicks off. Back to Sam]

   Got to fly. When I get back we'll go over a few clean tech

ACT TWO; SCENE FOUR

opportunities. There's one, Agile Tech, that's really got me hard- got a process that turns waste plastic into fuel--but we'll talk. I'll update you as soon as I hear anything on our deal.

SAM: Great, It calms people's nerves.

ERIC: You got it, guy.

SAM: I'll get the check to you for the additional shares.

ERIC: Perfect.

[They embrace.]

BLACK OUT

ACT TWO; SCENE FIVE
THE LOFT - DAYS LATER

Sam enters. They greet each other with a subdued kiss.

SAM: Hi.

KAREN: Hi.

SAM: I thought you were coming back tomorrow?

KAREN: Changed plans. I tried you on your cell. You didn't pick up.

SAM: I've been running like crazy. How was the visit?

KAREN: All right. How are you?

SAM: Good, good. I just got a text from Eric, The approval is moving ahead at SEABEC.

KAREN: So everyone is going to get their money back?

SAM: Many times their money back. Solar closed today at thirty-seven

KAREN: Do we have to put up more money?

SAM: No, Karen. This is good news.

KAREN: I have some bad news--that's why I came back early.

SAM: Listen Karen, I'm sorry I know I've been preoccupied with--

KAREN: I told Charlie about the Xerxes deal and how we were waiting and waiting to hear from SEABEC. He said he had a friend of his, a lawyer at his firm, who does a lot of work with SEABEC and he'd ask him to see what he could find out--

SAM: Why the hell are you involving Charlie?

KAREN: The lawyer checked. He told Charlie that there is no hearing about a Xerxes buy-out by Solar Systems on SEABEC's agenda. Nothing has even been filed.

SAM: He doesn't know what he's talk-

KAREN: Sam, he's just relaying the information.

ACT TWO; SCENE FIVE

SAM: Anyway, it's fucking bullshit! Why is your asshole brother involved in my business?

KAREN: Because you're living with his asshole sister. Charlie contacted one of Xerxes' co-founders, Jon Chen, who told him there was no hearing before SEABEC and Xerxes was not being bought by anyone.

SAM: Total bullshit!

KAREN: Chen told Charlie that Eric Deveraux has no financial interest in their company.

SAM: I was fucking there! Eric took me to their offices. He introduced me to Jon Chen.

KAREN: Did you discuss the deal?

SAM: We weren't supposed to because we were hip pocket investors. Come on, Eric was CEO of the fucking company.

KAREN: Five years ago. Chen said he resigned after six months and sold them back his share options. He hasn't had anything to do with Xerxes since except-

SAM: Come on, Eric's office is there.

KAREN: Except they rent him office space. Charlie offered to look at the deal papers and give us a recommendation about what we should do.

[Sam is on his iPhone...]

SAM: This makes absolutely no sense at all..

[He goes to leave. Karen blocks him.]

KAREN: Sam, Charlie said not to have any contact with Eric.

[Sam pushes Karen out of his way and exits.]

BLACK OUT

BIG MONEY

ACT TWO; SCENE SIX
ERIC'S HOUSE - LATER

Eric packs. Moving boxes are scattered about. A Red Bull is balanced on one of them. Sam enters.

ERIC: Hi guy, what brings-

SAM: Where are you going?

ERIC: I finally found a loft in the city I like, a few blocks from you. No worries, I won't invite myself to dinner--too often. You look a little fried, wassup?

SAM: Karen dumped some weird news on me.

ERIC: Don't keep it all in, guy, it's your buddy you're talking to.

SAM: Karen told her brother about the deal being hung up at SEABEC.

ERIC: No longer, SEABEC's full commission just gave its approval. Game over!... I was just going to text you.

SAM: Karen's brother says the Xerxes buy-out by Solar Systems isn't on SEABEC's agenda.

ERIC: They don't put buy-out approvals on the agenda--to protect against insider trading. But this is not good--Karen talking to her brother. There are a couple of delicate dances ahead and we don't need any stumbles.

SAM: You just said it was, 'game over'.

ERIC: I know what I said, Sam. The stock transfers are happening as we speak but there is also currency exchange rates, conveyance, titles, insurance all of which have to be negotiated and signed off on so we can close-

SAM: You said we had closed.

ERIC: O.K. What's the bug up your ass?

SAM: Karen's brother called Jon Chen. He said Xerxes is not involved in any buy-out deal with Solar Systems and you

ACT TWO; SCENE SIX

haven't been an investor in Xerxes since you resigned as CEO. I need to know what's going on Eric. FUCKING NOW!

ERIC: Jesus Christ, Sam, are you trying to blow the deal! Jon is going to be furious about this. You give out no information. None. Not even your middle initial to unknown parties when you're going through a buy-out. Jon's been calling me all morning. Now I know what it's about. With all due respect, Karen's brother has fucked things up. Big time! We could get stripped of our shares!

[Sam pulls out his iPhone...]

ERIC: Who are you calling?... Talk to me guy...

SAM *[Into phone.]:* Xerxes Technology...Connect.

ERIC: Sam, don't fucking compound this shit storm--You visited the company. You met them...Talk to me guy!

SAM: We never talked about Xerxes being bought by Solar Systems-- Yes, hello. This is Sam Garcia. I have Eric Deveraux on the line for Jon Chen. Returning his many calls. Sam offers Eric the phone, who takes it and breaks the connection.

ERIC: Sam, things have become complicated. I should have told you earlier. The Xerxes buy-out hasn't been happening for awhile.

SAM: It's a fucking scam!

ERIC: No, no absolutely not, Sam...I say that truthfully. I should have told you earlier that we shifted to other investments but the money's there.

[Sam steps toward Eric who backs up, knocking over a stack of shipping cartons. Sam is in Eric's face, threatening.]

SAM: I want it back! All of it. All we gave you. Call Kelly. Tell him we're coming to get it from his fucking bank or I go to the FBI.

ERIC: Sam, you don't want to do that. Believe me...We'll get your money back but you got to work with me. You bring in outside parties the only people who will see any money are lawyers.

SAM: You knew exactly what you were doing every--

ERIC: Easy Sam, easy. We need to focus on the money. We work together it's yours, no worries we can dig our way out of this but if the regulatory agencies get involved, the first thing they do is freeze everyone's assets.

SAM: No Bullshit. No delays.

ERIC: I'll make you whole. You can count on it.

SAM: And everyone else. Everyone's made whole.

ERIC: No worries, no worries, I'll have it for you but my bad, Sam, I should have reached out to you earlier. What happened was I thought I had my interest secured in Xerxes through a guy on the board who said he was going to sell me an option for five million shares, part of which I sold to you and the Matrix Group but that deal didn't ultimately happen so I put yours and the Matrix Group money into other investments. Believe me guy, we have some good plays out there. Better than Xerxes by far. Millennium Technology, remember we talked about it? And there are two social media start-ups that we have money in that are dynamite. We're going for the low hanging fruit this time.

SAM: O.K. Sell them and give us our money back. This is over . Eric. Game over!

ERIC: Sam, let me tell you how we will work it.

[Sam tries to interrupt]

Just listen--We'll let people know that the SEABEC thing has gone ahead but there's a few month's lag time. Make them understand their cash is as good as in the bank. Then

ACT TWO; SCENE SIX

we'll brief them about Millennium Technology opening up to new investors--and the two social media start-ups--we'll offer them the same deal we gave them on Xerxes with the money they made from the Xerxes deal.

SAM: No way this is going to happen. I'm not-

ERIC: Sam, you give them your confidence they'll buy in. If necessary we can even pay out a little interest on their investment. I've done some research on your Matrix Board. They may drive Priusses but their portfolios are high octane. We haven't even reached the mother-lode

SAM *[Losing it.]:* You're a con man aren't you Eric? A fucking con man!

ERIC: I thought we were over this shit but O.K. I'm a venture capitalist. Sometimes we cross lines to make things happen. When it works you're the second coming and when it doesn't people call you a con man or worse. But make no mistake all of us cross lines.

SAM: No they don't, not unless they're fucking thieves!

ERIC: How about signing Karen's name to your loan papers? Does that make you a con artist? A thief?... I don't fault you for it, I'd have done the same.

[The reality of the situation sweeps over Sam.]

SAM: Why didn't I see it? Why!...

ERIC: You wanted the money so you cut corners. We all do it so stop whining and man up. Sam, the way you raised cash for the Xerxes deal was awesome. I repeat that; Awesome! We work together we can make Millennium as big as that. Eric puts his hand on Sam's shoulder.

SAM: No!

[Sam violently knocks Eric's hand away sending him sprawling on his back. Eric's sits up, wiping the blood that trickles from the corner of his mouth.]

BIG MONEY

ERIC: Sam, you're too smart a guy so don't be stupid. We either work together on this or we go to jail together--Get it, guy?

[Sam, devastated by the reality he faces covers his face with his hands.]

BLACK OUT

ACT TWO; SCENE SEVEN
THE LOFT - LATER

Sam enters. Karen goes to him.

KAREN: I was so worried, Sam. I was afraid--

SAM: How could I have been so stupid. So fucking stupid.

KAREN: Others believed him too.

SAM: I vouched for him. I gave everyone confidence... Why didn't I know, Karen, why didn't I figure it out?

KAREN: Who wouldn't trust someone who hands them sixty thousand dollars.

SAM: It all made sense; everything seemed so right. Like we deserved it.

KAREN: He was brilliant, Sam. Found what you wanted and convinced you it was yours to take. I believed him too. It wasn't only you, Sam.

SAM: You were suspicious.

KAREN: I thought he was a jerk but not this. Nobody suspected so don't put it all on yourself.

SAM: Why didn't the lawyers know? I'm sure as hell going to find that out.

KAREN: What did he say when you confronted him?

SAM: He said he invested the money in some other start-ups.

KAREN: How could--

SAM: Maybe it's bullshit, I don't know. I destroyed everything. Everything!

KAREN: Everyone knows what you've done for Matrix.

SAM: I put all Matrix's reserve fund into the deal.

KAREN: But the board agreed: It's the board's responsibility too.

SAM: I didn't tell them.

KAREN: Oh Sam.

SAM: I have to find a way out.

KAREN: We have our home We have our baby--soon. We'll get through this together.

SAM: I used the loft.

KAREN: What? What do you mean?

SAM: I put it up as collateral for the loan we needed to cover the grants. Karen I'm so sorry.

KAREN: But it's in both our names?

SAM: I signed for you.

KAREN: You forged my name?

SAM: I'll get it back, I swear I will, Karen. This idea Eric has--I know he's a scum--

KAREN: Please, Sam, how could you do that to us. How could you?

SAM: Nobody would put up the collateral. Carl Boyce was going to do it then he backed out. Becky Clemons. Others too. Nobody would step up. I tried to get Eric to put it up or one of his friends--what a joke huh? I just couldn't pick up the phone and tell people sorry we can't pay you the grants we promised. I didn't see any alternative. Eric said I could just sign the loan papers for you. I'd have the grants covered and we were going to make a million dollars.

KAREN: How?

SAM : I used our savings too--as a private investment.

KAREN: I can't believe it.

SAM: Eric said the deal would close before we even had to pay interest I didn't think you'd ever know.

KAREN: What was it for? Wouldn't I know about that?

SAM: What?

KAREN: The million dollars you were going to make. What were you going to do with it?

ACT TWO; SCENE SEVEN

SAM: Me and Eric talked about going in together on some deals. I was going to use it for capital. Pretty funny.

KAREN: ...Sad. It is really sad.

SAM: I'll get it back--all of it. This Millennium stock deal Eric talked to me about it earlier. There was an article in 'Business Week' ...

KAREN: What happened to you Sam?...

SAM: I believed him. Everyone did. You did too, right? And I went out on a limb--I shouldn't have but I did.

KAREN *[Angry tears.]:* Don't you understand, Sam, It's us! We believed in each other we trusted each other. How could you take that away for money? You sold everything for money!

SAM: I wanted Matrix to grow, to succeed. What's wrong with that? And for us too. You wanted the land in the country- a house. We can work our way out of this Karen... It's not pretty but there's a way we can do it. Eric's plan isn't so bad. We just have to convince--

[He goes to her but she turns her back, opens her phone and places a call.]

SAM: Who are you calling. Don't tell--

KAREN *[Into phone.]:* Hi. I'm coming over...I'll tell you when I get there...

[Back to Sam.]

I'll come by in the morning tomorrow and get some clothes. Please don't be here.

[Karen grabs her coat and shoves the baby blanket in her bag Sam watches, desperate, She gathers up other necessities, keeping her back to Sam as he pleads...]

SAM: Karen, please, we'll talk this through--Please, I know we can. I'll get the money back. You just have to give me some time--Eric's a scum-bag--I know that but we have to work with him, it's our only chance. I swear to you I'll get the money back. I--

[Karen whirls around, facing him.]

KAREN: Fuck the money! I don't want anything, Sam, except what's gone --what we were. Our life! It's gone --destroyed for money; for stinking fucking money! And the worst and saddest most pitiful thing is you don't get it. You don't get it because you've turned you into him!

SAM: What about our baby? Please for her sake, Karen.

KAREN: Right now, I don't even want her to know you.

[Karen pushes Sam out of her way and exits. Sam's cell phone rings. Sam goes the window and looks out as the phone goes to message.]

ERIC [O.S.]: Wassup guy? Having a little make-up sex?

[He laughs]

Listen call back ASAP. We need a meet on the Millennium deal. I was thinking Zekes' Thursday? Give me a shout. Ciao.

END OF PLAY

www.ingramcontent.com/pod-product-compliance
Lightning Source LLC
Chambersburg PA
CBHW022104090426
42743CB00008B/709